jD is an award-winning writer/director and a stand-up comedian. Growing up with three sisters in a one-bathroom house, jD's imagination became his sanctuary. Taking apart pens to see how they work and undressing his sisters' Barbie Dolls to see what was underneath led to his passion for storytelling and women.

This book is dedicated to my mother, who taught me how to entertain; my father, who taught me how to tell stories; and my sisters—Karen, Nancy and Pam—who grounded me and taught me how to behave, how women think differently than men, how women are much stronger than men and to value shoes... especially when they are on sale.

jD Shapiro

THINK LIKE A MAN

The Only Guide You'll Ever Need

AUSTIN MACAULEY PUBLISHERS™

LONDON • CAMBRIDGE • NEW YORK • SHARJAH

A CIP catalogue record for this title is available from the British Library.

ISBN 9781788233194 (Paperback)
ISBN 9781528953313 (ePub e-book)

www.austinmacauley.com

First Published (2019)
Austin Macauley Publishers Ltd
25 Canada Square
Canary Wharf
London
E14 5LQ

Foreword

As a psychiatrist, I have never liked self-help books. You might think that sounds like a competitive or even sour-grapes-based opinion. It is not. Rather, as one who has been steeped in human tragedy and has had to navigate the murky waters of the human condition, I resent a book that promises 'cures' or easy answers to unraveling the indescribable complexity of human beings. Well, then I happened to come across a book by jD Shapiro named *Think Like a Man, a* treasure trove of wit, insight, and understanding on issues vital for happiness.

Mr. Shapiro has created a blueprint for relationships with clarity, eloquence, and at times bawdy humor. I found it mildly quirky, but all the more fun for its quirkiness. The book is nothing less than couples counseling for a fraction of the price. It bills itself as a guide for women who want to understand men and net the right man. Well, it does that and so much more. In my judgment, it is as important for men to read as for women. It is artful, respectful, and true. Moreover, it's served up in a masterfully funny way that does not in the least detract from the importance of the content. In fact, it renders the content all the more readable and digestible.

Read this book, have some laughs, take the advice to heart and you will have a more satisfying romantic relationship.

Martin H. Karasch, M.D.

Interactive QR Tags

https://youtu.be/oWxCzhMyC1A

DCT Comedy: JD Shapiro "I MUST BE CRAZY"

QR tags allow you to interact with the text and view video content on your smart phone. Simply scan the image using any barcode scanning application, and your phone will automatically open the videos. If you do not have a smart phone, the URL is included below each tag.

Contents

My Mission Statement

"The significant problems we face cannot be solved at the same level of thinking we were at when we created them."

– Albert Einstein
(One of the world's most brilliant Theoretical Physicist. Best known for The Theory of Relativity, and his snazzy hairdo)

ALBERT Einstein's quote is here to better prepare you for my mission statement, which is what I want to achieve for you in this book.

What Einstein means is that in order to solve problems, this includes the most important problem to solve, that being how to make your life happier, healthier, and much better, you need to, you must shift your energy. If you think at one level, you stay there. For example, if you think life sucks, that is the level you are at, the energy you are in and is what you will bring to yourself. If you go to a higher level, that being said, "How can I find a man I love and who loves me and wants to be with me for the rest of our lives," that is the energy you draw in and thus where you can now find better answers to better questions. All you need do is put those answers to practical use.

Among low energies are; hate, fear, prejudice. High energy; love, laughter, calm, courage.

This might sound like a bunch of mystic mumbo jumbo, but I assure you it's not. We are energy. Plug us into the right socket and, like a current, we thrive. Plug us into the wrong socket and we will burn out. In our case, those "sockets" are the questions we ask ourselves, and how we then act upon the answers. Einstein knew this. Thus, the reason he was a genius. He thought of the questions that would raise him to a "higher energy". You have the ability to do this. Yes, inside you lives a dormant genius. Geniuses still must work hard at their chosen field and will fail if they don't push through the times they are temporarily defeated. But if you choose to, you can use your genius to learn the truth about men and use it to gain a happier life.

All you need do is change the level of your energy to tap into a higher level of consciousness. Or, in man grunt, which is often sport speak, "Raise your game". Now to my Mission Statement:

To create a candid and empowering instruction guide for women, that outlines the truth about men, so you have the knowledge needed to think like a man, get a man and do it in a way that makes you both happy.

Because imagine what the world would be like if we were all less lonely and happier.

Footnote

"The truth will set you free. But first, it will piss you off."
– Gloria Steinem
(Founder of Ms. Magazine. Feminist.
Trailblazer Game Changer.)

I know 'footnotes' normally go at the end of a book, but (A) I'm dyslexic so I don't stick to the rules and (B) I wanted to write a footnote upfront to let you know that I'm going to include some foot-in-mouth notes.

I'm doing this because the only way to truly understand anything is to understand how it works. To understand how men work and *why*, I have to be 110% honest with you. This means I'm going to bust certain present day 'norms' and challenge many 'politically correct' issues when it comes to men and women. Therefore, I am going to piss you off.

But if I am not totally honest, you won't have full instructions on how to land a man and this book will fall short, like so many before it. More importantly, you will fall short of your goal of being in a happy relationship with a man you love and who loves you. This is the last thing I want to happen, so you have my word that I will NOT pull any punches and that I will show you how to think like a man, the truth about men and why these truths exist.

I want you to know how much I appreciate you taking the time to read this book. I know you could be doing many other things, including reading other books on this subject—dare I say, none with this particular point of view and none that will help you as much. There, I dared say it!

I think when you are done, you dare agree.

Mansplaining Man

SOME of you are going to accuse me of mansplaining. You'd be kind of correct. I say "kind of" because I am, but I am MansplainingMan... a subject I know better than you. Why? Because I am a man. Can I explain a woman as well as a woman can? No. No man can. And no woman can explain a man as well as a man can.

It's important that I mansplainman so you understand us men. This way you have the best chance of using your innate powers, and his innate weaknesses to land the man you want and do it in a way that makes BOTH of you happy. I'll keep saying this because I want it to stick. I'll say things you know but need to imprint into your minds, hearts, and souls. I'll tell you things you don't want to hear because you need to hear it to accomplish your goals. And I'll give you new information to help you get into a lasting, healthier relationships with men.

If you get mad at me, you can toss this MANual at me because you think it's not right for me to be MansplainingMan, you can do so and continue to fight windmills. You can see all the power and controls you have unused and miss out on secrets you want to uncover. Or you can allow me to mansplainman and use Mother Nature and all your talents to empower yourself and get your reward: a happy and healthy relationship.

Not surprising to me, all the men who read the book loved it. They all wanted to give it to their girlfriends or wives. What surprised me was only one woman wanted to throw it at my head. The rest were incredibly positive. The words they said most to me about this book were, 'Helpful', 'Funny', 'Educational', 'Read in one sitting' and 'Empowering'. I'm very proud of this, especially that they felt it was 'Empowering'. I'd love it if I can help someone in some small way bring out the power they already had inside of them.

Just sayin'.

Part I
Basic Training

Secrets Revealed

"The closest a man will ever get to Heaven on Earth is by being with a woman."
— Unknown

I'm giving away secrets that if we men admitted to, might get us into trouble. Actually, they aren't secrets at all. They are truths, truths that were beaten out of us for some right and many wrong reasons. These truths will help you land a man because the biggest truth is, *YOU HAVE POWER OVER MEN and have the ability to use that power to get the man you want to commit.*

Many of you already know this. But most of you don't know how to use it to your full advantage. If you did, you wouldn't need this or any other book. You'd already be in the kind of relationship you want to be in. And women would be in control of the world and in many more powerful positions than men.

Why do you think we men have such a strong need to control the TV remote? Deep down, although we will never admit it, we know it's one of the few things we can control.

You can manipulate a man for your gain—AND his.

When I say 'manipulate', I am not using the word in a negative way. Orthopedists and chiropractors manipulate bones back into place, so the patient can heal. However, the word "manipulate" has negative connotations, so I will use the word 'operate' more often, which seems to have fewer negative connotations, even though I'd rather have a doctor manipulate my bones than operate on them.

Incidentally, don't you find it interesting that words that help you get what you want, like manipulate starts with the word "man"'"? Coincidence? Maybe. Or perhaps, men are just that easy to maneuver.

If your aim is to learn about manipulating or maneuvering a man to use him and discard him, please dispose of this book. The secrets I reveal and truths I tell are *very* powerful and give you instructions to get what you want from a man.

As you read on, you will learn these truths and how you can use them to your advantage. Some of what I'm going to tell you is plain ol' common sense. That being said, if common sense were more common, then people would do sensible things more often.

One truth is JUST ABOUT EVERYTHING A MAN DOES IS TO GET A WOMAN. We'd still be in caves if it weren't for women.

Another of these truths is: MOTHER NATURE GAVE ALL WOMEN THE TOOLS NEEDED TO ACCOMPLISH THE GOAL OF GETTING A MAN *AND* KEEPING HIM.

What she didn't give women was the instructions. Another truth is MEN HAVE CERTAIN *INSTINCTUAL HABITS* THAT YOU CAN USE TO GET WHAT YOU WANT FROM THEM.

We humans are habitual creatures. Both good and bad habits are hard to break. *You will become a great habit he won't want to break.*

As Confucius said, "Men's natures are alike, it is their habits that carry them far apart."

You want to become his habit, so he carries you far past all the others and into the honeymoon suite.

Now that you have a book that reveals secrets, tells truths, and gives instructions… you're on your way.

Thinking Like a Man Is for All Women,
Not Just Those Looking to Land a Man

"I think women are foolish to pretend they are equal to men; they are far superior and always have been."
– Sir William Golding
(British novelist, playwright, poet, and Nobel Prize winner. Best known for his novel "Lord of the Flies".)

I have lived on the west coast and east coast of America. In the past six years, I've done a lot of traveling in Europe and spent over a year living in Spain. Prior to that, I did some traveling to South America, mostly Buenos Aires once a year for five years, where I'd spend up to three weeks there. I learned that Think Like a Man is universal. Although cultures, customs and languages are different, sometimes vary, the core of a man is not. And because of this, women can "weaponize" yourselves by USING (not just reading but *using*) what's in this book to empower yourself to get what you want from a man. These secrets that are powerful truths will work the same for a woman in Utah as it would in Madrid.

Sadly, there are some countries that will ban my book due to its ability to empower women. Some men fear women learning the knowledge within this book because these "men" need to be the king of their domain! The master of their house! The rulers of the world!!! These men are called "Shitbrainfuckheads". Or, much more elegantly put by someone much, much more elegant than me, *"Let's be very clear: Strong men—men who are truly role models—don't need to put down women to make themselves feel powerful. People who are truly strong lift others up. People who are truly powerful bring others together"* – Michelle Obama (One of the classiest, smartest, and bravest First Ladies of The United States). Luckily, most men aren't Shitbrainfuckheads. And the majority of men will WANT women to learn the truths within this book and USE THEM because it will make their lives better.

Although I mainly wrote this for women seeking a healthy, long-lasting relationship with a man, I have come to realize (because I've been told by several women who have read this book), that Think Like a Man is for ALL WOMEN. Times they are a-changing. With the #Metoo, #Timesup and many other great movements aimed at empowering women and shaming men who deserve to be shamed the timing of this book couldn't be better! I guess I'm lucky it took me so long to write. I hope that women learn so much about men that they use this information "From the bedroom to the boardroom." (I don't mean that literary as you will see but you get the idea). So even if you have no desire to be in a long-lasting relationship with a man, or to have any kind of physical relationship with a man, you can use these truths to learn how to gain advantages over any man; In business and in EVERY other area of life that you must deal with a man. Thus, making your life much richer, much more enjoyable, much happier and much, much better. Over time, you will see just how powerful these truths are.

As you read on, you're going to think, "Hey, Mr. Grunter, many of these chapters have nothing to do with the work environment! I'm not doing that at work for no man!" You'd be right. You shouldn't do them. Or should you? I don't want to get ahead of myself, but I will say read between the lines of those chapters. Understand that no, you should never be told nor expected to make coffee when you're an equal or above the man asking. Nor should you do it if that isn't in your job description. The idiot man who asked should apologize and get it for himself. So no, you shouldn't do it. But on certain occasions, should you? Read on and find out before you throw this book at my head. I will say this; in the movie, *The Godfather*, during a meeting where Don Vito Corleone, the most powerful of all the Don's, he is the one who pours the drinks for the other Don's. As I will point out in another chapter great king knew to bow before another king, because it gave them the advantage to get what they wanted. It is the QUEEN in chess who has the power to move in all directions and is the most powerful piece on the board. The king is the weakest and often it is the queen who protects the king. In fairytales, it's the opposite. Until recently. Fantastic movies like *Frozen* and *Wonder Woman* don't have men coming to the rescue. It is the women who are the heroes. Yes, times they are a-changing. For the better for women and I hope this is just the tip of the iceberg (*Frozen* pun intended). As I point out—the truth is that the inherited instincts of a man have not changed much in the history of human evolution.

Read on. Enjoying learning the truth about men and use the very easy techniques in this book to Think Like a Man and unlock and gain control of that incredible inner power you have as a woman to get what you want from a man.

If Men Came with Instructions, You Wouldn't Need This Book

"I, with a deeper instinct, choose a man who compels my strength, who makes enormous demands on me, who does not doubt my courage or my toughness, who does not believe me naïve or innocent, who has the courage treat me like a woman."

— Anaïs Nin

HAVE you ever seen one of us knuckle-draggers trying to put something together without reading the instructions?

You look at that idiot and shake your head, because you know he's going to need to use that instructional guide at some point. More than likely the thing he's putting together is going to either fall apart or not work as well as it could.

It's kind of the same when we men watch you ladies try to operate us.

When men say they will never understand women, what they are really saying is, "I will never understand why women *don't understand men.*"

We know we're simple creatures with simple wants and needs and figure we should be easy to operate.

Unfortunately, Mother Nature didn't give you an instruction guide that reveals the inner workings of a man and key insights into what makes us men tick.

Think about it. If your car broke down and you knew how it worked, had instructions to guide you and the tools you needed to fix it, you'd be on your way. Same goes with getting a man and keeping him.

The good news is, unlike a car, which can be very complex, a man isn't. So, the instructions are easy to follow. The great news is, you already have the tools. The best news is, if you follow the instructions I give you in this book, you can use your tools to your advantage *and* his.

Because he'll love you for it.

Xs and Os: Gaining an Advantage

"Love does not begin and end the way we seem to think it does. Love is a battle, love is a war, and love is growing up."

– James Baldwin
(Bestselling author, Leader in the fight for civil rights)

GETTING a man to commit is not laying a man, dating a man, or ending up in a relationship that lasted as long as the last one. It's not about winning one game, getting through the playoffs and into the championship. It's about winning that championship.

As you can see, I will be using sports analogies. One reason I do this is that any sport, in its purest sense, is a great metaphor for life. Another reason is to help you understand men better and help you to speak his language. I am NOT saying women don't understand or love sports. I've met almost as many women like men who do, some women much more knowledgeable than many men, some better athletes. But I found that most women don't use sports as an analogy— a language to understand men and get a man.

For example, when a woman sees 'XO', most of you think 'Hugs and Kisses'. Most men think sports. 'X' and 'O' is what a coach draws on the blackboard to give strategies in order to create a game plan that will lead to victory. Another reason I'll be referencing sports is so those of you who aren't sports fans can get extra 'points' (which I will be talking about later), with a lot of men if you know a little 'sport speak'. In sports, this would be called a 'Triple/Double'.[1]

In any sport, you have a goal you want to reach. To attain that goal, you must use your individual skills and talents to the best of your ability. Talent is given to you by whatever higher power you believe in. They become SKILLS only when *you work to make them better.*

In the 'sport' of landing a man and keeping him, the man you want to get is both your opposition and your goal.

Again, *the man you want is the opponent you need to overcome; in order to get the prize, you want to win. Him.*

Ben Hogan (one of the world's greatest golfers), once said, *"There are three ways to beat somebody. You outwork them. You out-think them. And you intimidate them."*

When it comes to men, you already out-think us. The 'work' you'll need to do to outwork us, you will soon find out, isn't that much work at all and isn't very hard. As far as intimidating a man goes, most men are already intimidated by women. That's why they do what they can to keep you out of business, politics, etc. They know you will far outperform them. However, in this context you're going to "intimidate" in a good way. You'll do this by getting under his skin in a way that he likes you so much under his skin, he's afraid of you not being there. That's how powerful this book is. Follow these principles, and you will have a man worried that you could leave him.

> These truths will give you strategies, so you can create a game plan that will lead you to victory. One of those truths is to learn how men process things and how our 'simple' minds work.

WHY?

If you know the 'why', the 'what' becomes much more palatable.

---

[1] When a basketball player scores double digit points, double digit rebounds and double-digit assists, it's a 'Triple/Double'. When I say it in this book, it means you get more than one benefit from doing something I suggest.

When I say men's minds are 'simple', I am not calling men stupid. I'm saying a man's wants and needs are much simpler than most women understand.

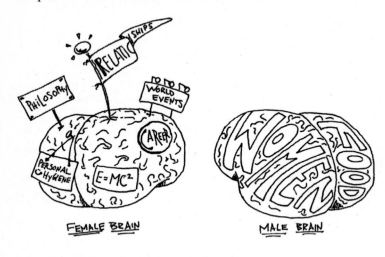

FEMALE BRAIN   MALE BRAIN

To create a winning game plan, you must:

- *Study your opponent and learn as much as you can about them.*

By doing this, you learn their strengths, their weaknesses and how you can use *both* to your advantage.

- *Be honest about your strengths and your weaknesses.*

By doing this, you can exploit your strengths and, either stay away from your weaknesses or even better, *turn your weaknesses into strength.*

Roger Federer, one of the greatest tennis players ever, at one time (and this is hard to fathom if you've ever watched him play), had a bad backhand. The way to beat him was to go after it. He thanked all the players for going after his backhand because it forced him to work on it—until it went from being a weakness to a lethal weapon.

NOTE: When I say a 'game', I'm talking about using a game plan *with integrity and honesty.* I am not talking about playing surface games and using a bunch of *The Rules* or becoming a *Why Men Love Bitches* bitch. Those books and books like them do women a disservice because those kinds of games don't lead to happy, healthy, and long-lasting relationships. Those parlor tricks will never truly get into a man's bloodstream... which leads to his heart—the place you want to be.

Great champions are extraordinary at taking the long view. They are aware of what's been working and what's not. Chances are you are not aware of this when it comes to getting a man. I plan to change that.

All women get rated the very moment a man makes contact with her. (Just like, I'm guessing because I'm not a woman, you rate us the moment you come in contact with us.) We rate using a point system, usually from one to ten. We men love a point system. It *simplifies* things for us. We don't have to think so hard. A man can grunt '21 beats 16'. (Golf, which was invented to confuse and frustrate, is the opposite.) Even when it comes to women, we 'score'.

Hmmm... interesting that we call it 'scoring', don't you think?

Your first points come upon the moment of contact. Whether that be over the phone, through an email, when he first lays eyes on you in person, or on Facebook, an online dating site or, maybe, for some of you a TV show or Movie. (Reality shows seem to attract some women to some men and not being a woman, I can only guess why) From that moment forward, you either score more points or lose them. It's just not as black and white as it is in sports.

He thinks, "She complimented me in front of my friends, I'm going to bring her flowers next time I see her."

You think, "He brought me flowers—he must be up to no good!" (Okay, okay, hopefully, what you're thinking is, "That's really sweet of him.")

If you're not, and you're constantly thinking he's up to no good, 1. Why are you with him and 2. You're going to lose major points if you act upon that feeling and you're wrong. (I'll address that in a coming chapter).

Points add up. Even small ones that might not seem like much; which is why when you get to "What you need to do"

29

section, you will read both big suggestions and ones where you'll think, "Come on, is this really that important for me to do or be wary of?" Yes. Great athletes are great athletes because they understand that even the smallest nuance can make a huge difference.

I cannot stress this enough. So, I'm going to stress it again.

Even the Smallest of Nuances Can Make a HUGE Difference.

This is not only true in sports but also in life. A ripple in a lake can create oceans of possibilities.

Great athletes do the 'littlest' things that make a huge difference so they can *gain an advantage*. Michael Phelps (who, at the time this book was published, is the most decorated athlete in Olympic history having won 23 gold medals and 28 overall) worked on leg strength more than most swimmers do. He won his seventh gold medal in the 2008 Summer Olympics by 0.01 of a second. He certainly understood that any advantage he could gain, no matter how little, was worth gaining. *Any*.

In the 'sport' of landing a man, the competition is fierce, more so for women than for men. Because of the plane, train, automobile, and internet, there are countless numbers of amazing women for men to choose from. I'm sorry to say it's harder for you ladies to find an amazing man; one who isn't in 'the "idiot" pool'. But, those amazing men are out there. And when you find one, you want to keep him. So, it helps tremendously to have an advantage *going into the game*. (Many boxers talk about how they win or lose the fight in the locker room—before the fight has even begun.)

Conversely, you can also lose points. Lose too many points and the man you want will disengage.

I'm going to teach you how to score points and not lose points so when he tallies them up, you have a winning score in the 'PRO' column.

Scoring these points is in your control. The reason you want as many positive points as possible is even a few negative points can sink you. Why? Because subconsciously, a man is looking for reasons not to marry you. Let me repeat this…

A Man Is Looking for Reasons Not to Marry You

All of us men have a belief system that has been pounded into us, by no one in particular. He's a good 'catch'. Best way to get a man is to 'trap' him. If a guy gets married, he's 'biting the bullet'. 'Taking the plunge'. 'Tying the knot'. You know, like the executioner does after he puts the noose around your neck.

Here's my absolute favorite worst statement we men hear all the time, 'Bachelor party = last night of freedom'.

You want that man to associate marriage and you with words and phrases like, 'I won't find any better woman out there, ever', 'She makes my life great', 'She makes me feel whole'. You want your man to feel like he's never been as happy and as free as he is with you in his life because now *he has a partner; a teammate he can build a life with.* This is infinitely more satisfying than spending a life 'chasing tail'. (A term men use that ironically means to spin around in circles and get nowhere.)

Yet, 'chasing' is a better term than being 'caught' because one rings of freedom and the other doesn't. See my point?

Put in plain and simple guy grunt, no man gets married because he's tired of 'chasing tail' or never having anyone to answer to. They do it because they feel they have someone in their life that touches them deeply, makes them better, and makes life better for them. Inside, men know that age will eventually turn all those random women into forgotten memories and having no one to answer to eventually turns into being the old dude in a nursing home who gets excited about the nurse that comes in twice a day to change his diapers just so he has someone to talk to. Knowing this subconsciously means that he wants to avoid that—and the only way to do so is to be in a committed relationship.

By the time you are done with this book, you are going to learn what you can do to get into his subconscious *and* conscious. You're going to learn how to become his Most Valuable Player (MVP).

You're going to make him to feel there is no one out there he could trade you for because there is no one better for him out there. As I said, *you're going to become that habit he won't want to break.*

The more you're willing to do, the more of a habit you become. The more of a habit you become, the more *advantage you gain over your competition*, other women and the man you want to land. As I said, you want that advantage, *you need that advantage.*

To give you that advantage, I'm going to go back to the basics, or as coaches like to call them, 'fundamentals'. You must *master your basics* to become great at what you are doing. They are the foundation upon which all else is built. The Fire is about as basic as it gets. Yet without it, we wouldn't have *survived.*

One of those basic fundamentals is worth repeating. You can take control and guide us men in the direction you want us to go... if only you know how.

You will, by the time you're done with this book. This book contains everything you need so you will know how to get from point '**A**' to point '**B**ride'. It gives you the advantage you need to score points. And by scoring points, you narrow the playing field until it's down to one...

You.

The Power of the Pussy

*"You are the one that possesses the keys to your being.
You carry the passport to your own happiness"*
– Diane von Furstenberg
(Formerly Princess Diane of Fürstenberg,
fashion designer, champion or women's rights)

WE are in the midst of a great change for women. An incredibly important and well overdue one. As I write this there is #Metoo, #Timesup and I'm sure others will come, and I hope they all sustain.

Women have had enough, rightfully so, by the way, men have been acting since MAN made religion was invented. All religions were created by men except Wicca, a female religion that men feared so much they burned witches (women with power and intelligence). Men wrote in all the major religious texts and in that Dogma, women were below second-class citizens; a man's property to treat with and do with as he pleased. ALL this needs to change. Unfortunately, many of these things will take time to change. However, change is a coming thanks to the many brave women stepping forward with their stories of abuse as well as those who suffer silently but add to the fuel of the movement because they have been there and had enough. More women in The USA are running for political office than ever before. Women in an office with power positions are finally, I think, helping other women move up the chain. Yes, I said "finally" because for too long that hasn't been the case and was part of the problem. Go ahead, hate on me, and kill the messenger. But the truth will live on until it's openly talked about and understood why this happens and how we can fight ingrained instincts we have to change this (I talk about this in an upcoming chapter). Be afraid you men of incompetence in the workplace, you monsters of evil who think women can be groped or mistreated just because you're a man in power or just a man. Your days are quickly ending you predatory monsters that have bullied, feared and/or shamed women into silence. Your day of reckoning is finally coming. Thank The Universe!!

Too often women don't know their value and power because it's been beaten out of you since the moment you were born and continues to happen throughout your life. Most of the time is subtle messages. After religion, a lot of those messages come from advertising telling you what you should look like, think like, dress like, be like, etc., etc., etc.! As you know, most advertising decisions are made by men. It's 2018 and it's still this way! But now, in part due to the person in The White House (well I think it's a person), and fantastic reporting by Jodi Kantor, Megan Twohey and Ronan Farrow about Harvey Weinstein, they somehow broke the dam and got women AND men to hear and, more importantly, believe. Rose McGowan (an actor, singer, writer, victim, survivor, and brave activist) has been screaming to the deaf for years about "Monster Harvey" and others. Turns out that Ms. McGowan is not only incredibly brave and very smart but she's not crazy like media outlets controlled or fearful (same thing really) by Monster Harvey wanted you to believe. She has become one of the main voices and leaders of this incredibly important time in history. Like many women, she is using her pain to help lead the way down a path that she has said she is not sure where it will take her. All the incredibly brave women who have come forward, as well as those still living within their silent pain because they aren't ready to come out for a variety of reasons no one has the right to judge, are making a difference. I bring up the silent women because too many of you are living silently in pain. Hopefully not because of a man who abused you in some way, but possibly because by not living to the fullest of your incredible potential, there is a void you feel, cover-up quickly and move on, never being able to run fast enough to fill that void.

Please do NOT mistake the silence of a victim/survivor

with the silence of an enabler, or those that know something and say nothing. To me, in some ways, these people are worse than the monsters that perform their vial act of using power and feeling powerful to hurt women. The enablers are complicit. They are also monsters. *"The world will not be destroyed by those who do evil, but by those who watch them without doing anything."* – Albert Einstein

I hope the path many women are now on takes ALL THE WOMEN OF THE UNITED STATES AND THE WORLD into a new world, one where women can no longer be shamed nor silence into submission, one where those who commit these heinous acts and those who are complicit by enabling them are imprisoned, and even better, a world where acts of violence, groping, sexting without permission and all men-inappropriate behavior becomes much, much, MUCH less frequent. I'd love to say never happens again, but I live in a reality of a world were human nature is filled with many flaws. You will see the flaws of men as you read on, and how you can use them to EMPOWER YOURSELF.

Too often strong women with an opinion, a voice that differs from the current norm, are treated by men, and women, the media, religion, etc. as "crazy" or outliers. These strong women aren't treated with the intelligence they have with something that needs to be said and a voice that needs to be heard. These cowardice men and women do all they can to invalidate women who speak out because they fear them. These cowardice men and women fear their power to effect change. So, they "burn them at the steak". Not literally, the way they did in the past (although I strongly suspect many would love to) but with effective, well researched and thought out propaganda "trials" that do, unfortunately, negatively affect public opinion about these women. The list of women who have suffered from this from the past to present day is, unfortunately, way too long to list. However, you know many of them, and if you don't you should. Google; it's a beautiful thing! Women are rising up, seeing they are worth more and deserve better. Women are demanding long overdue change and will no longer be "grabbed by the pussy" and just take it.

I bring all this up in a book that focuses on how by Thinking Like a Man you can get one you deserve because My NUMBER ONE GOAL is to EMPOWER YOU. I've said it and I'll say it again and again. Because you have the power. You really, REALLY do. You have the power and deserve to be in a relationship with a man who loves you for all you are, and all you are not. A man who brings out the best in you because he cares deeply about you. A partner. One that can help you be happy. Yes, you make your own happiness, but it helps if you surround yourself with people who are on your side and not make you feel less than you are. It helps more if one of those people is the man you love. It's time, long overdue, for you stop allowing men, society, religion, societal "norms", stares, gossip, rumors, what other people think and their opinions to stop you from being all you can be, and you can be a hell of a lot. YOU CAN affect positive change in your life, and by doing so, you affect positive change in the entire world.

Change can take time. Or as Gloria Allred (a women's rights attorney, earth shaker, groundbreaker and trailblazer who has been fighting for women's rights way before most and way before it became "popular") more elegantly and accurately said, "*Male privilege and entitlement are dying a very painful death; no one gives up power without a struggle.*" In this change, we need to remember words matter. Ms. McGowan talks about moving the needle by 10%. (FYI: I don't know nor have ever met Ms. McGowan. I am bringing her up several times because I truly admire her strength and what she is doing. She is not only an inspiration to women, but to me, and I hope many men. Any women I mention in this book is an inspiration to me for reasons you'll understand as you read on and get to know me. Ms. McGowan happens to be, as I write this, talking truth to power and "making people uncomfortable". Her words. I for one think that is a great thing!). It might not sound like much but it's actually seismic and once moved 10%, it breaks down huge barriers and can move on from there. On that note, how we phrase things and many sayings we have to make a difference. They not only become part of our vernacular they become part of our socialized DNA. Ms. McGowan said, *"I want to reframe words, logic, and conversation."*

So, let's start that today.

As I said words matter. That the pen is mightier than the sword and, possibly for the first time in history, the pen is now mightier than the penIS. In the USA women make around $.27 cents on the dollar LESS than a man makes doing the same job, and probably not doing it as well. Women of color make less. We still have people who don't understand it's not all right to touch a woman unless she MAKES IT CLEAR it's okay. Or say inappropriate things. Yes, women like compliments. But she doesn't need to hear what a great rack she has or great ass UNLESS you're in an intimate relationship with her. Then by all means compliment her body more than you do and more often. Women don't want you to send inappropriate pictures. Guys, have you looked at your dicks? Move your fat fucking belly and take a look. She doesn't want to see it. Chances are, even the woman who loves you doesn't want to see it. That's why the "Off" switch was invented for lights. You ain't Michael Fassbender, and even if you are that endowed unless a woman ASKS you, she doesn't want to see Mr. Happy 'cause it makes her want to Ms. Puke.

Terms like, "You run like a girl" are beyond stupid yet said all the time. Go running with Flo Jo and let's see how you feel after she races by you. "You throw like a girl." Really? Try to bat against Lisa Fernandez and I guarantee you she will steam the ball right past you. "You hit like a girl." I double/triple dare you to say that to Cecilia Brækhus. And when you do please, please, pleaseeee let me know so I can be there to record her knocking your ass out when she hits you and share it on the internet with the world to show how stupid you are.

Right now, the term I want to change most is how we associate men and women with our genitalia, and how this term makes absolutely no sense what so ever. Perhaps what I am advocating for is not a big change, and perhaps one that won't move the march miles or the needle even close to 10%. But each step is a mile in the making.

The term I want to change is, "He (or she) has balls!" We all know what it means so I don't have to go into it much but to sum it up it means the person with "balls" has strength, guts and power. This makes no sense. NO SENSE AT ALL. The expression should be, "He (or she) has pussy!"

Yes, pussy!

Pussies are strong. Tough. Powerful beyond. They not only take a pounding, but they also want it more often. Granted the pounding usually only last two, to two and a half minutes, but it's still a pounding and that pussy loves it! Try pounding on balls. Within seconds the owner of those balls will be begging you to stop. Crying in pain. Never again wanting you or anyone to pound them (Okay, there are exceptions like Sadomasochistic balls, but those balls still don't have the strength nor power of a pussy.)

You don't even have to pound balls to cause the man who owns them to lose strength. Just hit them, lightly, and watch their owner crumple to his knees. I know a man who was roughhousing with a five-year-old. As they tussled in fun, the five-year-old giggling like crazy, he mistakenly kneed the man in the balls. This man went right to his knees and was in intense pain. This man—okay it was actually me, told/screamed to his nephew "Time out!!!" So much for pounding balls, they can't even take a knee from a five-year-old! This is why the more appropriate term "I'm busting your balls" exists. Balls are quite easy to bust.

Now let's talk about the strength and power of the pussy. First of all, strength comes in many forms. One kind of strength is to actually be soft (something men have a hard time doing or admitting, which I get to in later chapters why and how you can use this to empower yourself). Strength can be sweat. Strength knows when to hold tight and when to let go. Strength thinks before it acts. Not in every case, but in most. Balls can't do any of that. But pussies can (No, I'm not saying you don't want sex as much as a man. I am saying most women will consider many things, within seconds, before diving open. Men think of nothing else, even if given months). All balls can do is swing, hang and shrivel up. They can eject stuff out of them, then immediately convince their owner it's time to roll over and go to sleep. (Perhaps that's why another more appropriate term, "Bust a nut" exists. Sure, it's not literal. But most balls lack power and strength once they've performed their task in two and a half, maybe three minutes). But a pussy can take it hard and soft, some even eject stuff out of them, and pretty much most pussies want to take a short pause and then get right back to pounding. "Sleep time, Mr. Balls? Come on, I'm ready for more! Wake up you weak, powerless sack of balls!"

Another power of the pussy is, many pussies give birth. A pussy allows a much, much larger object or objects to come out of it. That's fucking strength! That's fucking guts! That's real fucking power! That takes serious pussy!!! And some pussies do this incredibly powerful and painful thing more than once!

A pussy can do way more powerful things than anything balls can do. That's right. Pussy to Balls: "Whatever you can do I can do better. Like a 1000 x 1,000,000 better." If it weren't for pussy power, strength and guts, humans would die out. Balls—remember to thank pussy for you being alive whenever and as often as you can.

So, let's make this change starting today: Never again and no longer say or write to a person that has courageous or powerful or guts or strength or some or all of those that they have balls. Tell them "You've got pussy!" Like I said, this isn't exactly a huge change, but it is a small step in enforcing in men and women that women have a lot more power and strength too few people give you credit for. It's a way to empower you because the fact is, most women are more resilient, grounded and in many ways, stronger than men; and all women have pussy!

So, journey forward and learn how to Think Like a Man so you can understand men. In the process of learning about us Grunters, you will empower yourself in ALL walks of your life. For those of you who bought this book because you want to be in a happy, healthy and long-lasting relationship, you will have a much, MUCH better chance of not only landing the right man, but also avoiding the wrong man. Because as vastly important as the women's movement is, you don't want to forget love. Love cannot be truly explained no matter how hard the greatest of the greatest artists, philosophers, scientist, writers, singers, and poets try. But it sure as hell is magical.

Part II

Why I Can Help You "Land" a Man

"The supreme happiness in life is the conviction that we are loved... loved for ourselves, or rather in spite of ourselves."
– Victor Hugo
(One of France's most important romantic writers)

WHY does a man who has yet to be 'landed' want to write a book on the subject? Simple. It makes me sad when I look around and see so many unhappy and lonely women wanting to be in a relationship and not knowing what they can do and how much power they have to turn that want into a reality. Then I got mad when I found out many women were trying to find answers in books that didn't ask the right questions. Too often these books have the reader listening to bad advice, and in some cases, harmful advice. As I mentioned, most men who want healthy and lasting relationships don't want to marry bitches. If he doesn't call you back right away, it doesn't necessarily mean "He's Not That Into You", and when a man behaves badly, it certainly doesn't mean it's your fault. Don't let Dr. Schlessinger or anyone else tell you otherwise! That kind of advice is not only mean spirited, but also disempowering to women. (By the way, there's a reason the term 'landing a man' exists. Like landing a plane, it's the pilot who is in control. When it comes to men, YOU are the pilot.)

Men might be from Mars, and women might be from Venus, but until we get to either Venus and/or Mars it's best to have an enjoyable and easy to read MANual here on earth to understand men and help you get the man you want.

Alohomora! You now have it. Use it wisely.

This book started out as a section in my journal. I was jotting down the kind of woman I'd like to meet; my wish list of what she'd be like. As I wrote, I realized that after I got past the usual things men think about—looks, sexual chemistry, sense of humor, etc.—I started to write LITTLE things a woman could do that would make a BIG difference. As this section in my journal grew, I realized that I was creating instructions that could be turned into an operating MANual.

Some of my male friends thought what I was creating was dangerous to us men. But I explained to them why it was important that women know these secrets and truths and how that would help us men get what we wanted as well. That's when they got mad at me, because I was wasting my time hanging with them and not writing this book... or as one of my male friends called it, "The Bible for women."

A lot of books are written by people who only do the research. In this case, I am the research. With all due respect to some doctors out there, (I'm from Jersey and Hell's Kitchen, so we say things like; 'With all due respect', 'Not for nothing' and 'Yo'), this is not something that can be taught to you by a person who learned theories in a classroom or by just doing studies.

It can't be taught to you by a woman, either. Yes, there are many women who have an understanding of men. But they don't have the entire story and can't get to the core of a man, because they are not men. They might be able to tell you how to get a man, but they can't tell you what he really, truly needs in order for you to keep him. So, unless a woman was once a man, a woman doesn't fully know what makes us men tick. And the advice given is either part right or all wrong. (Same holds true for a man writing a book about what a woman wants)

It also cannot be taught to you by a man who doesn't like nor respect women and doesn't have your best interest at heart. There are a lot of men who write incredibly stupid books that act as if women are not as smart as men, not as worthy and not as equal. They tell women they need to change and/or hide who they are in order to get a man. These men are called "Fucksticks," because they don't respect women, the power a woman has and a women's ability to do many things beyond what a man is capable of doing.

This needs to be taught by a man who cares about people, likes and respects women and has PRACTICAL experience. A man who has actually lived the 'catch me if you can' life.

You don't need an M.D., Ph.D., E.D.D., D.R.S., or D.D.S. to teach you what I'm about to teach you. What you need is empathy, respect, a C.O.C.K. and be willing to put that 'degree' on the line, which I am willing to do.

I am also is a very hard catch. I'm not saying I'm a good catch, I'm saying I'm a very hard catch. I'm part of a group called 'The Ungettables'.

That makes me the perfect guy to study with and learn from because I am a man who wants to be gotten, yet hasn't been. That might sound like a contradiction but it's not. Why? Because being an ungettable makes me the toughest opponent you can find. I know what it would take to 'beat' (get) me. If you can beat the toughest, you can beat the rest. For or example if you wanted to beat Serena Williams at tennis the best person to study with and learn from would be... Serena Williams.

By the time you finish this book, at worst you will further understand and embrace the innate power you have, not only in your personal life but in your professional one as well. You will also know how to land a man.

About Me

"For all its pains, love is what makes life meaningful. For men, as much as women. And maybe even more."
— Unknown

I feel you should know about me, your own personal knuckle-dragger, on this journey of knowledge and information.

Once upon a time, in a not-so-distant land called 'Jersey', I was born. By the time my mother had enough morning sickness, and both of my parents were over the thrill of diaper-changing, there were four of us. Three sisters and me.

Economically, we didn't have much. At times we were lower middle class; at other times we were poor. But I had riches that could not be measured in dollars. A loving family and a mother who was there for all of us 24/7. My dad was around when I was very young, then he wasn't, then he was, then he wasn't until he wasn't anymore. He just wasn't ready to be married. He was an ungettable. I say 'was' because he was happily married for the past 21 years until he passed away two years ago.

I don't tell you any of this to elicit any kind of sympathy. My dad attended all the important events. He taught me how to catch a football. I got my love of storytelling from him. I tell you this because I want you to know that I'm a man who was brought up surrounded by women, and because of this, perhaps, I have a better understanding of women, but more importantly—I have a better understanding of *the way women view men.* I see the mistakes women make and a lot of them have to do with not understanding how men think. Because we men are basic and simple creatures; we act a certain way and expect certain things from women... things that were instilled in us *before we were even born.*

As a man, I also know what men are willing to say, and what men really want to say. The two don't always go hand-in-hand. In fact, many times they don't.

For some reasons unbeknownst to me, I am considered to be a good catch. I've been told I look good on paper. Ladies, a puppy looks good on paper, until he becomes a dog and still is on that paper. I'm not a 'Type-A' male who can walk into a bar and have women throw themselves at me. I've been told I'm kinda cute and kinda sexy. (I have a strong feeling George Clooney and Chris Hemsworth don't have 'kinda' in front of those descriptions.)

I'm not 'Average Joe' either. At least, I don't think I am, but hey, you'd have to be the judge. I've been with my fair share of women, but I'm no Wilt Chamberlain.[2] I don't think Wilt Chamberlain was Wilt Chamberlain. I'm not bragging, I'm just saying that I've had experience with many different types of women. Enough to see that each woman is unique, yet all have one need in common:

The need to *SURVIVE*.

Ah, I bet you thought I was going to say 'the need to be loved'. Yeah, that's way up there, but survival is the thing we all have in common. As deep as love runs—and it runs deep—survival runs deeper. This is because if we don't survive, we can't love.

---

[2] Famous basketball player who claimed to have slept with over 30,000 women. According to my calculations, that would mean during his 15 year career, he would have to sleep with at least one woman before the game, another after the game and three during the game.

Oh Brother, Where Art Thou?

"Advice is what we ask for when we already know the answer, but wish we didn't."

– Erica Jong
(Writer of 'The Fear of Flying')

IF you have questions about a man's motives or truths, you can seek your girlfriend's advice, but you'd be much better served by asking a guy's advice. Birds of a feather know other birds of that feather.

Your girlfriend may also have an agenda you are not aware of. What if she's in a bad relationship or marriage? She might give you bad advice. Most of the time, she won't be doing it consciously, but remember, 'Misery loves company'. What if she just doesn't like your man? What if she does like your man?

You want to get advice about men from a man.

Here's the tough part: Your male friend can't have any other agenda than to want to be your friend and see you happy. There are a lot of guys out there who just want women as friends. They're called gay.

Okay, okay... There are guys who want to be just friends with women because then they have someone who can give them the female point of view. Nah, who am I kidding? Unless they're gay or your brother most of those guys are going to eventually want to have sex with you too, so their answers will be tainted. Okay, okay, there are guys you can and hopefully will be just friends with. But until you know for sure that it's just a friendship

Here's where I come in.

Besides being your guide and coach, I'd like you to also think of me as your brother. Not the brother who used to play jokes and torment you growing up, but the brother who cares deeply for you and whose one and only agenda when giving advice is for you to be happy and not to get hurt.

Women, who know me and come to me for advice, knowing I will tell them the way it really is with us, knuckle-draggers. Growing up surrounded by women, I am a lightning rod for my sisters, my female friends, their female friends, women who just met me—you name it.

I'm totally honest because I want to protect their hearts. To do that, it means I want them to know the truth about how men think, so they don't bury their heads in the sand, fall prey, and get hurt.

Also, I want them to see how *they can use these truths to their advantage.*

I do my best to be gentle with my advice, but at times, even a dove's wings can feel like razor blades. Sometimes, they want to kill the messenger. Sometimes, they listen. Sometimes, they don't. The times they didn't listen to my advice, they always found out that I was right. Not because I'm so smart but because I'm a man and I know of which I speak.

I want you to come to me through this book anytime you have a question. The answers are on these pages. Use this book, follow your gut, and you will never go wrong.

Part III

What You Need to Know

"Men want to take over the world. Women want to live in it."

— Unknown

SOME of you are going to skim this part of the book because you're anxious to get to 'What you need to do' section. Please don't.

It will enlighten you and give you the knowledge that will help you build a solid game plan.

The more knowledge you have about something, the more in control you are of the situation; the more of an *advantage you have* over others.

If you were a doctor, how could you help any of your patients if you didn't know how the human body works? Some doctors are general practitioners and others are specialists.

Think of yourself as a specialist, studying one specific thing so you can master him.

If Mother Nature Talks in the Woods, Does Anyone Hear Her?

Don't Fight Mother Nature—Work with Her

"Courage is the price that life exacts for granting peace."
— Amelia Earhart
(First woman to fly the Atlantic, Trailblazer)

WE men like to think of ourselves as kings; most of us aren't even princes. Many of us are still toads.

Several studies indicate that men are born flawed. Our 'Y' chromosome is actually a defective 'X'. (Men are 'XY', women are 'XX'.) The 'X' chromosome carries three times more genetic material than the 'Y'.

I believe the 'Double-X Factor' is the reason women live longer, male babies have a higher mortality rate, women are less susceptible to disease and don't complain nearly as much as men do when they get something as tragic as the common cold. (I suggest you watch this BRILLAINT short [1:36] created by the British comedy Show "Man Stroke Woman about a Man-Cold". It truly captures us men and what you have to deal with!

https://www.youtube.com/watch?v=VbmbMSrsZVQ)

The Double-X Factor is probably why women are the child-bearers and why most men thank their mothers whenever they accomplish something. Sure, without our fathers we wouldn't exist. But without our mothers, we wouldn't have SURVIVED.

Men plant the seed. Women need to be strong enough to incubate the baby, birth the baby, feed the baby, and eventually, marry a big baby.

If women didn't have this strength, survival of our species would be in great jeopardy. More than likely, we'd be extinct. So, women are stronger than men. Women are also for the most part, much more 'in tune' than men. We can be clueless when you aren't. I'm not making excuses for us men, I'm telling you this so you can work with the information.

I'm going to teach you the ways and whys we men think. As I said, once you know the 'why', then 'what' becomes that much more palatable. You might not always like the way men think. Check that. There are definitely going to be many times you don't like the way men think and you could give a damn why men think that way.

When this happens, you have two choices: You can try to change the world and fight Mother Nature as well as human nature, or you can use a man's instinctual attributes to *your advantage*.

Again, YOU CAN USE A MAN'S INSTINCTUAL ATTRIBUTES TO *YOUR ADVANTAGE*.

There are many different theories about how long women and men have roamed the Earth. Many religious people believe it's been for about 6,000 years, while many scientific experts say we could date back as long as six to eight million years ago, with a species of humans called Ardipithecus (I go with the scientist). Our instinctual attributes (which form habits), go back a very, *very* long way.

Our strongest instinct is THE NEED TO *SURVIVE*. So strong is our fear of not surviving, we do things in life that we think will guarantee our survival at the expense of living a fully enriched life. We'd rather exist than live

The innate things that make us tick have pretty much stayed the same since our beginning. We still have a tailbone. We have tonsils and an appendix, and other physical items we no longer need. We also have inner emotional attributes that cannot be seen. One of those is a man's instinctual view when it comes to women and what we expect of them. (As you have your views of men and what you expect from us.)

You can take the boy out of the cave, but you can't take the cave out of the boy.

Much of what we did in Cave Town (for both women and men), cannot be written, spoken, beaten or forced out of us, regardless of what 'modern' society, men's groups, women's groups, advertisers, movies, TV shows, magazines, politics and the PC Police say or do.

The world around us keeps changing, but in many ways, we don't.

Great surfers know not to fight Mother Nature because if they do, they'll wipe out. They use her innate power; in this case, the ocean to their advantage. By doing so it is the surfer who controls the ocean and gets the ride of her or his life.

So instead of fighting Mother Nature when she says, "Because I said so," be a surfer, go with the flow, and work with her. Because, despite all of our many flaws, you still want to be with us.

And we men are thankful for that.

Men are Dawgs

We Are Habitual Creatures. Use That Innate
Quality to Train Your Man

*"The great pleasure of a dog is that you may make a fool of
yourself with him and not only will he not scold you, but he
will make a fool of himself too."*

– Samuel Butler
(American Author, From his 1912 novel, 'Notebooks')

I could state the obvious when I say 'Men are dawgs', but I
am going to turn the obvious into... well, the obvious.

Dogs can be trained.

They can be trained to come when you call, sit, roll over
and... Am I talking about dogs or dawgs?

You might be thinking, "You can't teach an old dog new
tricks." You actually can—but why work so hard when it's
much, much easier to take the old tricks and make them work
for you.

All animals, not just the men, are slow to break habits.
Especially if those habits are six to eight million years old.
This is *good news*. This is how you can train a man. NOT by
changing all those years of habits but by using those habits to
your advantage.

Again, you can *TRAIN A MAN BY USING ALL THOSE
YEARS OF INSTINCTUAL HABITS TO YOUR
ADVANTAGE.*

I'm sure you've heard of Pavlov's dog. The dog that
they'd ring a bell for and then feed—until whenever they rang
a bell, the dog would start to drool.

Need I say more?

Okay, perhaps I need say.

Robert M. Pirsig said in 'Zen and the Art of Motorcycle Maintenance':

"When a shepherd goes to kill a wolf, and takes his dog along to see the sport, he should take care to avoid mistakes. The dog has certain relationships to the wolf the shepherd may have forgotten."

True. But the biggest difference between dog and wolf is dogs have been *domesticated*. Although they still have many instincts of their forefathers, they realize that they have a much better chance to *SURVIVE* and a much happier existence if they stay in one place where they are treated like a king. They have shelter. They are fed, walked, bathed, bragged about, and loved.

Sure, you might have to discipline your dog every now and again, but if you stick with it much as Pavlov did for his dog, you can use a man's instincts and habits to become a habit for him.

By doing so, he might not slobber every time he sees you—but on the inside, he'll be hungry for you.

But Really, How Happy Is Gloria Steinem?

> The Women's Movement Did Some Harm to
> Women and Our View of Relationships

"People do not like to think. If one thinks, one must reach conclusions. Conclusions are not always pleasant."

— Helen Keller
(Deaf and blind, she became proof that anything is possible)

LIKE I said up front, I am going to have some 'foot-in-mouth' notes. This chapter title alone should do that trick. I named it this to get your attention. I also did it because I wanted a good excuse to buy a new alarm system for my place.

Upon first glance, you might wonder what this 'history lesson' if you will, has to do with getting a man and keeping him. It will further help you understand what goes to the basic core of what men really want and think but don't speak. It will help you see why understanding a man's instinctual habits are so important in helping you understand how you can and why you should make yourself one of his habits.

Mother Nature has given you many tools and many ways to gain an advantage and get what you want from a man. Tools that aren't used as much as they used to be because some people would consider them 'old-fashioned thinking'. Some people might even say that these are not the ways of a 'modern' woman and this is 'regressive' thinking. Some would say that they are not 'PC'.

But, you're not some people. You're you. And you deserve to be happy.

So—I put myself on the line now for you because you took the chance to buy this book. I have to take the chance to tell some hard truths that coming from a man might bring me your wrath.

I'm not a chauvinist. A chauvinist believes men are better than women. This kind of men is also called 'Fucksticks'.

There's a reason women are called 'our better half'. But, there are major differences between men and women.

Men are better at certain things that are not overtly obvious. Women are better at others. I'm not sure what the big deal is. Both sexes are lacking. That's probably another reason we like being with each other... it fills gaps (literally and figuratively).

Let's for a moment think about all the many ways, big and small, men and women are different. From the silly to the not so silly, here are some examples: A man's need to control the TV remote. A woman's need to own as many pairs of shoes as possible. A man's need to never ask for directions, even when he's lost. Women feel the need to nurture us. Men feel the need to protect women. Women like to be cuddled. Men like to complain to other men about cuddling, even though we kind of like it—some of the time. Your need to create. Our need to destroy. Your need to talk things out. Our need to take time and find space. Your need to be held. Our need to give advice. Your need to feel like a woman. Our need to feel like a man. There are many more examples, but I know you get the idea.

I like to believe that most men are not chauvinists. However, I know most men are still part Neanderthal. (This is why after we get married; women make most of the important decisions.) Because men are part Neanderthal, we want and expect women to do more things for us than women want and expect from men; except in the area of money. In the United States, even though it is estimated in over one third of married households, it is the wife who is the bigger breadwinner, men still want to be the bigger breadwinner AND are expected to be by most women. Yes, I said expected to be by most women. According to Money Magazine, University of Texas Psychologist David Buss has found that, across cultures worldwide, women value 'good financial prospects' more highly in a potential partner than men do. This was the case even among feminists.

Why do most women expect their man to be the breadwinner? Is it because most women are gold-diggers? Hardly! It's because it's *instinctual*. It goes back to the cave when men hunted and provided the food and women did all the rest. From day one, men were the providers, women were the nurturers. Argue all you want, but we were born that way.

Admitting truths about human nature can be difficult because, as I have said, they're not always pretty. But if you admit those truths, you gain knowledge, which you can use to your advantage. Somethings you can use to your advantage are things the women's movement told you were to your disadvantage.

To understand what I mean, let's take a trip back in time:

From just about the very beginning of our existence, and throughout most of history, there have been more women than men. Men had more choices in Cave Town. Once chosen, we'd conk Dream Girl on the head, grab her by the hair and settle down with her for the rest of our natural lives; which was about another eight years. Maybe nine. Okay, we might not have actually conked and grabbed, but isn't it kind of ironic that many times when a little boy likes a little girl, he pulls her hair? As I said, old habits are very hard to change.

In Cave Town, both men and women shared in different but equal responsibilities. Women still doing more of the workload. Like it is today. His career was to provide food and protection. Her career was to do everything else, including birthing the child, raising the child, ensuring the human race would continue. Then, one day, we left Cave Town to find a "better" world and things started to change. The word 'Man' was used every time both men and women were talked about in the Bible. Even though it's supposed to refer to both sexes, 'man' became a more important word than 'woman'. The Bible, and pretty much all *man*-made religions has always treated women as second-class citizens. Or worse, as property. Still to this day. All religions were written by men. The one exception is Wicca, which is why men were so threatened by a female based religion that witches were burned at the stake. Religion dogma is one of the main reasons women in today's society still get paid less than a man, still get abused by men while the laws allow it to happen, still live in "a man's world." I hope this finally changes and with the #Metoo, #Timesup and all the other movements happening now this hopefully will ASAP. This conversation is a book for another day. Back to how to get a man...

When the barter system ended and the monetary system began, more things changed. You now had to have money in order to live and women still had to be the ones to carry the babies in order for our species to survive.

As I've stated, the world around us changed. We didn't.

It made sense for men to leave the house and get a job because it is not easy to work when you're pregnant and then have a baby to take care of. A lot of you are thinking, "Are you kidding me? That's what I do every day of my life, Mr. Knuckle-dragger!"

I know.

As Jane Sellman said, *"The phrase 'working mother' is redundant."*

Especially in society today.

The problem is no one called raising a family 'real' work, or a career, or even a job because there was no pay for it. We live in a world obsessed with putting a $$$ figure to just about everything, and falsely believing the more money someone makes the more they are worth. So, no pay = no respect for the work that was involved. Or the person doing the work. That person being women.

Women started to become more educated and aware that they had more value than they were being told. Also, divorce became more prevalent. One of the many by-products of divorce was that women needed to make their own money in order to—*SURVIVE*. Yet, women were not given the same business opportunities as men.

The Women's Movement was started to help ensure that women wouldn't be treated equally and would be afforded the same opportunities in life that men received. It was designed to free women from the shackles of bigotry by the uninformed (and just plain stupid) men, who viewed them as not only second-class citizens but as property. (Sadly, some 50 years later, women make about $.77 cents on the dollar to what a man makes for the same job. And chances are she must work twice as hard to get to the position) Women wanted more, and of course, deserved more. In the process, they put too much pressure on themselves to be 'superwoman'.

In a perfect world, a woman would be able to have a very respected career that being raising a family if she so desired. Then, after the kids were off and running, she could go into the out of house workforce, if she so desired. (Let's say, for argument sake, "Politics". So, the country finally has a better chance of becoming the great nation we aspire to be). This one-time career housewife would be someone in high demand because she just succeeded in the toughest field there is. There would be bidding wars for her! There would not only be room at the top, but the bar would also have risen because she is the top! I truly believe if they ever did a reality show pitting housewives against presidents of corporations and/or countries, the housewives would win hands down.

The demands women made then and still make now are 110% just. Anyone who argues differently is a fool beyond. But with all due respect, here is where the Women's Movement also did some harm:

1　It devalued women who 'just' wanted to be housewives. It actually allowed men to reinforce the feeling that the job a woman does at home is insignificant and not a job at all!

2　It lied. It said, "You can do and have it all (without feeling stressed or pulled in every direction). A husband! A baby! A career!" (That's true once you get married since most husbands are all three.)

3　It said that cooking and many of the things women do for men is belittling to women.

But, men still want a woman to do certain things for them—emotionally, physically, and mentally—*no matter what societal changes are made.* It doesn't matter if you're a mother, housewife, celebrity, doctor, rocket scientist, lawyer, architect, Secretary of State, Speaker of the House or, hopefully, one day soon, President of the United States. Men still think like men and view certain aspects of women the way they did in Cave Town. It's *instinctual.*

Like I said, the world has changed, but we humans haven't advanced as far as we would like to think we have. We still go to war. We still hate out of fear. We still fear out of ignorance. We're still ignorant because we are too afraid of the truth. Like, say the truth about men and women and our instinctual differences.

The movement also challenged how men and women should act with each other. All these societal changes became confusing to men. And guess what? When you're confused you're not sure what to do, you get scared and so *your survival is threatened.* To not feel threatened, men tried to acclimate to survive in this 'new' world.

Sensible men understood women were his equal. Most men had no clue exactly what that meant. Women wanted men to be more sensitive. Men tried to be more sensitive but weren't sure exactly how sensitive they should be before a woman would think he was not "acting like a man". Women became certain that there was more to life than they had been reaping. Yet many were torn between having children and working while raising a child and wanting to be with their child, but also wanting to succeed in and out of the house workplace. Men became uncertain as to what their role now was in life. Men tried to see things from a woman's point of view and got headaches because their minds couldn't handle those complexities. Do we open the door for you or is that being sexist? Do we call you Miss, Ms., or Mrs.? Do you take his last name or keep yours? Do you keep yours and also take his? Do men make the first move or is it Sadie Hawkins Day every day? Do you want men to pay for the date and make more money than you at the same time wanting to be equal? Do men have to learn to cook or can someone please invent the fucking microwave? Am I saying we should go back to the '50s when many women mindlessly did their chores and Stepford Wives their way through life? NO! Not at all! I'm saying that even with all our societal and technological advances, we still have instincts that go back millions of years and *you should use those instincts today to get what you want now and for your future.*

So, why not admit that the world changes but many things about us humans stay the same? Why not use our own origins and understand our history to create a present that will lead to an amazing future?

Why not use your innate abilities and a man's own instincts and habits to get what you want from him, especially if it doesn't really take that much effort to do it?

I have no idea how happy Gloria Steinem is. I hope the answer is "VERY" happy. Although mistakes were made, and pretty much always are even when the cause if a good one and important one, she is an extraordinary person that helped make the world a better place for women AND men. But I can tell you with 100% certainty that it's time to stop fighting windmills, stop living someone else's idea of a PC existence and start understanding human and especially men's nature. Don Quixote lived a lonely life. And Eleanor Rigby should be a song that you never have to live.

W.O.E.

Women Get Catty—for a Reason

"I can protect myself from my enemies, God save me from my friends."

– Voltaire
(French-born author and philosopher, probably didn't have many friends)

WOMEN get catty. (Don't crucify me until I'm done. Then, you might want to crucify me, but at least I got to say my piece before you tear me to pieces, and I rest in peace.) Women trust each other less than you trust us men.

Am I lying? Or are you smiling because you know of which I speak?

I call this the 'Witches of Eastwick' syndrome; 'W.O.E.'

Some woman will take a good man away from another woman, even if it's her friend's man. W.O.E. Too many women in power won't promote other women. W.O.E. History states that Shakespeare was the first to say, "All is fair in love and war." I think it was Mrs. Shakespeare.

When I was dating Penny, we went to an event.

NOTE: In all examples, I've changed the names to protect, mainly, me.

Penny and I had been going out only about a month. We ran into Anna, a woman who I recently worked with on a movie. Anna was flirty with me and acted like Penny didn't exist. The conversation lasted maybe 30 seconds.

Penny got jealous and angry—with me. "She was flirting with you and you didn't do anything!"

"Uh, I introduced you, took your hand, and ended the conversation quickly."

"You introduced me as Penny. Not your girlfriend."

I didn't know we had official titles, and I apologized. That wasn't enough for Penny. Friends and business associates were nearby when this went down, and I was embarrassed. After that night, I decided to exchange Penny for better currency. A few weeks later, I got a call from Anna, who got my number from I don't know who, saying she heard I broke up with 'that girl from the party' and wanted to know what I was up to. Penny never thought to think that maybe Anna acted the way she did to push Penny's buttons. It worked! W.O.E.

A great sports example of W.O.E. is chess. In chess, you have to sacrifice men in order to get the king. Hmmmm… You sacrifice in order to get the king. His main protector is his QUEEN.

Interesting, don't you think? The King can only move one step at a time. He's kinda simple. The Queen can move anywhere and anyway she wants. She can run circles around her King and all other competitors. The only one she can't run circles around—the other Queen. She's her most dangerous competition. By the way, in cheese when the Queen is sacrificed for the King, she gives up her life.

All things considered, the 'sacrifices' I'm going to suggest to you in Part II, aren't so bad after all!

Superwoman Complex

Stop Trying to Change Him or Save Him.
You Can't.

"I have yet to hear a man ask for advice on how to combine marriage and a career."
— Gloria Steinem
(Founder of Ms. Magazine, Feminist, Trailblazer)

Exactly!

And ironic.

Gloria Steinem, in those two lines, summed up a huge, massive, humongous difference between women and men.

Those two lines also explain why women feel they need to be Superwoman. Trying to do it all; career, husband, kids is very difficult. It's ridiculous that anyone would expect that from you. It's unfair that you expect it of yourself. Superwoman could do a lot of things, but last time I checked, she wasn't married, she didn't have kids... and she didn't have much of a life of her own.

Which leads to every single Superwoman who wants to save (change) that man you want to be in your life. Most men don't want to be saved because they are happy with who they are, or, in many cases, scared to death of who they are not. He'll never admit that. Not even to himself. Most men have potential, and chances are, that potential will remain just that.

Being a hero can lead to a lonely life. In many cases, the mask they wear is to hide their own void. But that's like putting a Band-Aid on a broken toe. *Fill* your void with someone who deserves your love.

Superwoman wants to save the world. She forgets to save herself. She is lonely until she is saving someone else. But soon that someone has drained her and moved on. Then, once again, Superwoman is empty, alone, and looking for someone else to save. Anyone... but herself.

The Ungettables

Some Men Just Can't Be Gotten

"When people show you who they are... Believe them the first time."

– Unknown

NO matter how beautiful, sexy, intelligent, fun, caring, incredible, and amazing you are, no book is ever going to give you the tools to get an Ungettable. Unless it's a big enough book that you can smack him upside the head, knock him out, handcuff him to the bed, and keep him there forever.

NOTE: What amazes me is how many of you ladies, armed with all the information I am giving you, perhaps some information you have gotten from other books, magazines, talk shows, personal experience, etc. will still—STILL—try to get an Ungettable, knowing he's an Ungettable, thinking you, Superwoman, can change him. No one can be 'changed' unless they want to change and have a reason to change. Ah, you're thinking, 'I'll be that reason'. Maybe, but doubtful. Not because you're not an amazing person, but because it usually takes more than one reason for a person to 'change'— and it usually takes more time and effort than it's worth because generally, the outcome isn't very rewarding.

If you insist on not listening to this advice, if you still want to keep trying to change him, and you use the tools I am giving you, the one and only piece of bittersweet consolation is, like the ghosts of Christmas past, present and future, will haunt him until the day he dies... and you will be the one who got away.

But is it really worth it? I don't think so. Seems to be much more bitter than sweet.

Sure, sometimes you want to be around something wild! Untamed!! Dangerous!!! But don't make those times the time you decide you're ready to get serious with a man. If you do, you'll be Wile E. Coyote chasing the Road Runner, and guess what? Like Wile E., you'll never ever catch him. Meep! Meep!

Life has many inexplicable things. One of them is something I am sure you've heard before: "When you close a door another one opens."

That's why I'm including this 'don't go there' chapter.

One of the keys to learning how to get a man is knowing when to cut one loose. You have to know when to close a door before your heart gets too involved and your soul gets drained. By closing that door, you are now open to meeting the right man—one who actually wants to be gotten by you.

In order to close a door, you have to really dig deep and be honest with yourself (sooner rather than later). Not an easy thing to do because too often we want to kill the messenger. And in this case, the messenger... is you.

In *We Married Margo*, a movie I directed, when Tracy and Jake are breaking up, Tracy says, "I wasted the best years of my life with you."

Jake's response is: "What are you talking about, you're 25 years old?"

It really doesn't matter how old you are, if you're with a guy you know is not going to be gotten (or isn't really that interested in being with you, or isn't right for you), you're just wasting time. Move on. Don't let fear stop you from what you need to do in order to live a life and not just exist in one.

Although I'm an Ungettable, I want that to change. I want to be gotten. Do I mean it? Yes! Am I capable of it? I really hope I am—but I don't know if I am. I hate admitting this about myself. Not as much to you but more to me because I really do want to fall in love, get married and build a life together with someone special. The question still remains, am I capable? I won't ever know for sure until I actually get married. That's the 'Catch 22' with an Ungettable. It's like playing sports. You can practice by yourself all you want and think you're great, but until you get into the game, you really don't have a clue.

I do know this: If I met a woman that I had chemistry with and she possessed 75% of what I suggest in this book, I would marry her because I can't imagine wanting any other woman to spend my life with. If I were stupid enough to blow it, she would haunt me forever.

I tell you this about me because many of the Ungettables will tell you they want to change. They will mean it, but they still might not be able to go through with it. As I have said, I want to protect your heart. Although a resilient muscle, it's an incredibly fragile one. I've had it broken—most of us have, many more times than once. I don't want you to go through that again. How can you tell if an Ungettable really means it when he says he wants to be gettable? You find out as much as you can about his PAST PATTERNS and watch his PRESENT PATTERNS with you. That old saying, "Action speaks louder than words" was, and always will be true.

If he's still doing the same old 'Not sure I can commit, give me a chance' song and dance—save you some time and heartache and move on. This guy is an Ungettable. He's not just not right for you, he's not right for any woman who wants to be in a serious, long-lasting relationship.

Bond. James Bond

Find Out If He Really Is the One for You
Before You Decide That He Really Is the One

"The difference between 'involvement' and 'commitment' is like an egg and ham breakfast: the chicken was involved, the pig was committed."

– Unknown

WHEN you first meet a man, he is on his best behavior. He is auditioning and he's saying what he thinks will get him the 'job'.

This is not unique. All men are auditioning when it comes to the beginning of a relationship. (I know women do as well.) And we are great auditions! We make Robert Downey Jr., Will Smith, Sydney Poitier, Paul Newman, Jamie Foxx, and Daniel Day Lewis COMBINED look like chumps.

He'll tell you how beautiful, or sexy or smart or amazing you are. He'll say things like; "I could melt in your smile," or "I've never met anyone like you," and if he's really creative, "I'd cross oceans to be with you." – Gary Oldman in 'Dracula'.

Sure, he can actually mean those things. But, "I've never met anyone like you before?" You just met! He's auditioning! He wants the part, so he's trying to steal your heart! He wants to show you he's great so he can get a date! He wants to get into your head so he can get into your bed!

You don't know if what he's saying is real. He doesn't even know if what he's saying is real. He might actually think it's real because Mr. Auditioned is talking through his penis.

By the way, most people think men talk through their penis. That is incorrect. It's a ventriloquist act. Except he's in control, and we're the dummy.

And the penis only has one goal.

Guys are auditioning from the very moment you meet. Sometimes, even when he's trying to meet you.

I was at the gym, working out near two women. Another knuckle-dragger was nearby. He was on his cell, grunting loud enough so we could all hear about his big movie deal and how Tom Hanks is going to star in it. Suddenly, his cell rings. The women nearby crack up—as did I, because he's been totally busted. This dumbass didn't even have the common sense to turn off his cell so it wouldn't ring while he was auditioning for these two women, hoping they would be impressed with his 'big movie deal' and want to jump into bed with him.

Mr. Auditioned will say whatever he thinks will work to get you into bed. That does not make him a bad man. That makes him a man. It is what men do. It is how we think.

Some men audition using facts, other men stretch facts, other men lie. For me, when I'm auditioning, truth works fine. But understand, I am still auditioning. For example, I like to get in as soon as I can that I grew up with three sisters because women seem to respond to that and I score points. Every man (and I am sure woman) has a 'bag of tricks' they know work because at one time in their life, they used it and it worked. And that's fine. It's part of the hunt.

Yes, I do believe in love at first sight. But I also believe in something Betty Davis said, "Love is not enough. It must be the foundation, the cornerstone, but not the complete structure. It is much too pliable, too yielding."

So sure, enjoy all the compliments. But before you go diving into the pool, give it time to see if it's real.

"Beware of Shark Infested Waters."

I was at a bar with my friend, Jack Ass. Jack was standing with a couple of women he had just met and waved me over. He said, "jD and I wrote a script together," (true). Then, he told them the script's name: 'Dumb and Dumber' (very not true). He has made me his wingman, so I don't say anything. (Men will cover for their friends—even when their friends are freakin' morons.) The women were suspicious. Possibly, because of the stunned look on my face when I found out the movie I wrote.

Jack panics and backtracks saying, "Well, we didn't get writing credit, but we did a rewrite."

They walked away.

Not all auditioners are this bad at it and blatantly full of crap as Jack Ass. Some men even enjoy the fact that you know the waters are shark infested and that they are the Megalodon. James Bond comes to mind. Moneypenny has a huge crush on 007. But she never lets it go any further than that. Why? I'm guessing she wants more than just a quick ride in the sack. So, she stays away from James because she knows his patterns. She knows it would be easier for Goldfinger to get him than a woman to land him. She did her homework.

You too can do some homework before or during the audition. Before the audition, maybe, there are friends or co-workers who know him. If no one knows him, there's Google and social media. These are beautiful things. Nothing wrong with using them and it's not sneaky. If you were interviewing for a job, you'd want to know as much as you can about the company and the person you're meeting with. Nothing wrong with wanting to know the same about some guy you're considering. You might find nothing, but then again...

During the audition, the way to do your homework is to let him speak. Although we knuckle-draggers prefer to grunt short answers to short questions, when it comes to talking about ourselves with a woman who actually wants to take the time to get to know us, we can be Mr. Chatty Cathy. Triple/Double by the way, because he's going to walk away feeling that you're a great listener!

You can't just listen with your heart. You have to listen past the dazzling smile, hot body, sweet attitude, romantic, smart, sensitive, rich, driven, charming, intelligent whatever man. You have to see past the carrot and see how many sticks there are, 'cause all men have sticks. Uh, excuse the pun.

He's probably not going to give you the full story and mess up his chances. He's still-hunting and hasn't landed his prey. He's in the game, but he hasn't won anything yet. Take it all with a grain of salt and listen closely, so you can also *hear what he's not saying*.

If he makes it to the callback[3] (or callback<u>s</u>), keep him grunting. His guard might come down quickly because he's used to doing all the listening. He'll be surprised you'll actually want to hear him speak. He won't even realize he's giving away 'state secrets', you can use to figure him out.

Again, LISTEN to what he says. I am amazed at how many times I've said from the start, "I have no interest in getting married at this time in my life and just want to have fun," and she would still think she could 'save' me. I realized it was because I said, "At this time in my life," and that gave hope. So, I stopped saying, "At this time in my life" and guess what? Yep, you got it! Many women still ignored the obvious. If any of these women had been listening, they would have seen, pretty quickly that I wasn't ready, and I was still carrying too much baggage. I was Humpty Dumpty and she should have Humpty-Dumptied me and moved on.

Yes, we all come with some kind of baggage, but it's better if you find a guy with a carry-on versus a steamer trunk.

Speaking of ex-girlfriends, if the man you want is still friends with an ex, she is a wealth of information. Don't alienate her. You want to meet her. She can become your best ally or your worst opposition.

There are times when men and women who have dated or even gotten married later realized they were better off as friends, and it forever remains that; a friendship. If he has an ex (or exes), he's friends with, who cares about what they once had? It's a 'had' not a 'have'. Befriend her. She is a hard drive full of information. You will learn much about him through her, AND you can also put any fears you might have to rest because you'll be able to see if she really is a 'had' versus a 'have'. As Marlon Brando playing Vito Corleone in 'The Godfather' said, *"Keep your friends close, and your enemies closer."*

During the first audition, remember that some guys are not full of crap. They are just bad auditioners because they are insecure with who they are and think they need to be

---

[3] When an actor auditions, if the casting director and/or director, producer or studio like them, they get called back in to see if they like them enough to give them the part.

something else. In reality, they are good people with big hearts so they might deserve a callback.

If, on the first date, Mr. Auditioner tells you he wants to get married and have kids one day? *"Warning Will Robinson! Danger, danger!!!"* He's saying it to bait you into bed. He's saying it because he senses that is what you want. Sure, he might want to get married and have kids one day. But he ain't saying 'with you'. Don't suddenly throw yourself in a wedding picture with Mr. Auditioner and do anything you're going to regret, like getting hurt.

This woman I know, Janet, met this guy Liar, who, according to her, said 'all the right things' on their first few dates. Liar actually said to her,

"I've kissed Cindy Crawford, I've kissed Cameron Diaz, but they are nothing compared to you. You are already in my heart. You are someone I could spend a lifetime with."

Janet bought it! She bought it knowing this guy made his living as an actor! She asked my advice. I told her run and never to look back.

She didn't listen.

After a couple of months of dating Liar, Janet came to me hurt and crushed and upset. Mr. Liar moved onto the heart of the next woman he could 'spend a lifetime with'. SHOCKING!

My brethren and sistren of film directors say 70% of making a film work is in the casting. Think about that. And use that before you cast a leading man into your heart.

Look past the audition, take the time to see if what he says and who he is, is for real. That way you can see if this is really someone you are compatible with—and if this is really someone you want to cast in your life… and who is capable of spending his life with you.

I Dream of Jeannie

All Men Are Looking for a Jeannie

"Falling in love consists merely of uncorking the imagination and bottling the common sense."
— Erica Jong

MEN think you can be Superwoman, but we want you to be Jeannie. Not something readily admitted because who wants to get slapped in the face? But I'm telling you the how men think; and you can bet your bottom dollar a majority of men have, what I call, The 'I Dream of Jeannie Syndrome'.

'I Dream of Jeannie' is a TV series about a man who lives with a woman. (You can watch episodes at Hulu.com.)

https://youtu.be/ShBFDFqlI0E
I Dream of Jeannie Season 1 Episode 1

She wears sexy outfits, grants his every wish… lets him be 'Master' of the house. She goes into her bottle when he asks so he can have his space. She does whatever she can to help him advance his career. She covers his back.

This is what most men want. Don't kill the messenger. I'm just telling it like it is.

If you ever watched the show, you know that Major Nelson ended up falling in love with Jeannie and marrying her. Hmmm... wonder why? Perhaps she knew that doing these things would score her big points and give her major results.

Perhaps, Jeannie knew that she had the real power—as did another woman named Samantha from another '60s show, 'Bewitched'. (Also available at Hulu.com.) It didn't bother them that every now and then, they took a little time to do some pampering and understanding—because it got them the end result they wanted.

Jeannie and Samantha had the real power in their shows because in real life, women have the real power. They knew that doing things for a man did not make them 'less than'. They understood that a smart king would kneel before another king, when he wants to gain advantage.

I have two friends, Eric and Joyce, who have been very happily married for 22 years. This is a second marriage for both of them and there is no end in sight.

Joyce once said to me, "I'm not the fantasy anymore. A beautiful woman can walk by Eric and capture his attention and imagination like that, but because of our relationship and what I do to insure it, it stays a fantasy."

When I asked her how much time it takes her to do all this stuff for him, she shrugged and said, "Really not much."

I then asked if she resented doing this stuff. She said, "No, Eric does a lot of stuff for me."

My response: "As much stuff as you do for him?"

After Joyce got done laughing, she said, "Come on, you know the answer to that. Of course not, he's a man!"

Yes, you might end up doing more for him than he does for you, but you will see most of the things I suggest aren't that difficult and/or don't take that much time.

A Jeannie is not a Stepford Wife. The man you are with should also be doing things for you. If he doesn't—dump him. This kind of man doesn't want a Jeannie—he wants a slave. This type of man is known as an 'assface'. A Jeannie is a woman who understands that by going back to certain instincts that still exist she can use them to her advantage to get what she wants from a man.

The instructions in this guide show you how basic a man's needs are, and how easily those needs can be met. You ladies have the ability to get that upper hand and 'control' your man in a way your man will never complain about. In fact, he'll actually be thankful to you! Was it not 'Beauty' who tamed 'The Beast'? Wasn't the mighty King Kong, who was as Neanderthal as it gets, putty in a woman's hands? If only you ladies would realize your power and that by being a Jeannie every now and then, you use a man's power 'against' him to your advantage. And you get what you want.

If only you were willing to spend some time being a queen who bows before a king—then you'd be his goddess. A goddess always trumps a king.

And a Jeannie got married to the man she loved.

Part IV

What You Need to Do

"You can kill all the messengers you want, but the message will still live on... Perhaps even longer."
— Unknown

IN this section, I'm going to tell you the things you can do to use his instinctual habits to your advantage, weaken his belief system, manipulate him in a way he'll like and become a habit in his life.

During some of the chapters, some of you are going to think, 'What did he just say I should do?' Thus, I will be telling you these things from a secure location, known only to me and the food delivery guy from Mulberry Pizza, who has been sworn to secrecy.

I totally respect that what little time you have left in a day after work, or taking care of the kids—or both—is precious. It's hard for you to find time for yourself, and yet I'm suggesting you find the time to do as many of these things as you can for him. Try to look at it as if you are doing these things for you as well—because, in the end, you are. You get the man.

Added up, these 'time consuming' suggestions are a fraction of what you might spend reading, watching TV, talking to your friends, or the big one that becomes more important than life itself—working on your career. Sure, getting to the top of your chosen field can be very satisfying. But, not nearly as satisfying as being on top of a man you can share your life with. "To love someone and have something you love to do is the greatest happiness there is".

I'm also going to tell you things you shouldn't do. Things that, for whatever reason, bother us men a lot more than they should, and probably a lot more than you know.

Ground Rules

*"There's only one way to have a happy marriage and as
soon as I learn what it is, I'll get married again."*
— Clint Eastwood
(Award-winning director, actor, and composer)

WHAT you do or don't do is up to you.
Each one of these 'Do's' and 'Don't's' has a point value. How
did I come up with this point value? On a scale from one to
ten, I had my own ideas about what things would be worth,
and I asked a bunch of my male friends what they thought.
Although sometimes my friends would say, "Dude, that's
worth a million points!" or "Man, that's negative 100,000!" I
am keeping the 'one to ten scale' to make it less confusing—
mainly, for me.

The point system isn't to be taken literally; it is to give
you an idea of how we men think and how we'd rate
something. Or someone. The main idea is for you to have fun
with it.

Here's an example, one that I hope becomes the norm.

One of the people I gave an early draft of this book to,
was Tim, a friend and business associate of mine. Tim read it
right before he was leaving for vacation with his wife,
Shannon. They went on an all-expense-paid trip, a trip
Shannon won because she was her company's #1 saleswoman
in the state. (She was also the breadwinner in the family).

While there, they met several other couples from around
the country, two married, one dating. When they were all
together, Tim decided to tell them about this book. This
opened up a friendly debate among the women and men. Two
of the women, who had said they would never do some of the

suggestions in this book, changed their minds. They instantly scored points from their significant other.

Now comes the twist I didn't expect.

Tim said the guys started to act differently with their ladies. There were hugs, kisses, compliments, holding out of chairs, opening of doors—things they had not done in a long time. All the women started giving their men points. One of the guys danced with his girlfriend for the first time since they met because he said he wanted to score points with her. Yes, you heard me correctly; *he* wanted to score points with her.

They would all playfully bargain, "I think this should be worth this amount", or "This is worth that amount", but, mainly and most importantly, they all had fun with it. They were both giving and receiving—by giving and receiving.

When I gave this book to Tim, I was just doing it to see if he agreed with me on the male point of view. He did. I did not expect him to tell anyone about the book, nor did I ever expect a group of men to unanimously get into the book.

Although I'm using the phrase, "For the six men, reading this book," hopefully more men will read it and respond and act towards their women the way these men did.

So, ladies, get ready to strap one on, 'cause political correctness is about to go out the door! I'll take the heat because I figure you all would rather hear some un-PC ways to get a man, than live a lonely life of politely masked lies.

Be a Fisherwoman

Reel Him in First, Then Once You Have Him
Hooked, You Can Keep Him

*"Whatever women must do, they must do twice
as well as men, to be thought half as good. Luckily,
this is not difficult."*
— Charlotte Whitton
(A Canadian politician and feminist, a leader in the fight to
protect children)

HAVE you ever watched a fisherman do his thing? For me, it's about as much fun as watching paint dry. But you can learn a lot from it.

Besides a rod, reel, and cold beers, fishing takes patience. Great fishermen know their adversary well and wear them down. They don't get so anxious that they yank and pull and end up snapping their line and losing that great catch.

Great fisherman picks the right bait to fish with. Many times, that bait is sparkly.

They go to a place *where the kind of fish they want will be there.*

Once the fish takes the bait and is hooked, a smart fisherman gives it plenty of line to run, then he pulls that fish in, gives that fish more line to run then pulls it in, then...

A great fisherman keeps doing this—until that fish is so well hooked that it is no longer willing to fight the inevitable. At that point, the fisherman reels in that fish and takes it home.

Be a fisherwoman.

Go to places where you can meet the kind of man you want to meet.

Again, GO TO PLACES YOU BELIEVE HAVE THE KIND OF MAN YOU WANT TO MEET.

Better yet, be a great fisherwoman.

Why hang out in place 'A' when the type of man you want hangs in place 'Z'? You're not going to a college kegger party to meet well-established businessmen. Not to say, some won't be there, but probably not the settling down kind of guy. You're not going to France to meet Brazilians. You're not going to Starbucks thinking you're going to get the same kind of meal you get at a wine and cheese place. To do so, wouldn't make any sense. Yet, I see women doing this all the time— biting into a pancake thinking he's going to taste like a filet.

I actually had two female friends recently complain to me about the kind of men they were meeting. FEMALE FRIEND: "I keep meeting cops and I don't want to date cops anymore."

ME: "Where do you normally hang out?"

FEMALE FRIEND: "A place called The Triple Inn."

ME: "The bar at 54th, between seventh and eighth? The one near the Manhattan North Precinct?"

FEMALE FRIEND: "Yes."

ME: (I stare at her then) "Go to the bar across the street. I heard they cater to firemen."

ANOTHER FEMALE FRIEND: "I'm done dating actors, but all ever I meet in LA are actors." (Sigh then)

"Hey, you want to go with me to this party at Leo DiCaprio's bar tonight?"

ME: I just stared at her blankly, then eventually blinked.

Choose wisely. Your time and money are better spent going someplace you can only afford to go to once a week that caters to the kind of man you want, than going to some local hangout all the time where you meet the same guys you have no interest in.

1   When you get to the place that has the kind of man you want, make sure he sees the bait: You. Many times, that means wearing sparkly things I know you know this but figured I'd say it anyway 'cause I'm a man).

2   When a man asks you out, he has taken the bait. You can then use the things I have suggested and will be suggesting in this book to make sure his audition is real and then hook him.

3   Once you KNOW he's hooked solid, you can reel him in, pull him onto the boat and into a journey that will hopefully last a lifetime.

Here's how a great fisherwoman would get her 'fish':

A great fisherwoman goes to places she knows the kind of man she wants to meet frequents. She meets a man, chemistry exists, date is made. First few dates, she sees he wasn't a fluke (or is that flounder), that the chemistry is real, and she wants to build upon that foundation with him. They start to build, and she has hooked him, but she's not sure how well that hook is into him yet, so she lets out some line. She does this by not talking about marriage, meeting family members, or having kids. In fact, she lets him do most of the talking. She knows that not only will he think she's attentive and interested, but she will learn about him and see if he is really the kind of man she wants to reel in. Triple/Double for you.

As she continues to date him, she reels him in some more, but slowly. How? She shows him how wonderful she is without putting any pressure on him to be with her. She does what I suggest in this book and sees that she has hooked him so tight; she doesn't have to bring him onto the boat because he's so happy, he jumps onto the boat himself!

POINT VALUE: No points go on his yellow pad for this one. However, this is worth an infinite amount of points for you personally if you are a great fisherwoman because you will get the man you want to get.

FOR THE SIX MEN READING THIS BOOK: I'm showing her things that she can do for you, so you better be doing things for her. The idea is to do things for each other, so it all balances out and... Okay, who am I kidding? It won't balance out. We're men. A woman will always end up doing more for her man. It's been that way from the moment we were conceived. They did everything for us those first nine months... and beyond. But guys—try to come close.

Spider-Woman's Web

Let Your Fingers Do the Talking

"One of the oldest human needs is having someone to wonder where you are when you don't come home at night."
– Margaret Mead
(Distinguished anthropologist and scientist)

YOU have a web you can shoot out of your fingertips any time you want to hunt for a man. All you need is a cell or computer and the Internet. Yes, I am talking about Internet dating. It is a pond that is well worth fishing in.

"Ewwwww." "Yuck." "That's so weird." "I'd never do that." "People on dating sites are losers."

A lot of people still say, hear and think these things when it comes to Internet dating. And a lot of people are still lonely yet unwilling to try a new approach. They are the 'losers' because they are losing out on possibilities that can lead to probabilities.

If you meet someone on a dating site, fall in love, and get married, you're a winner. If you just try this approach, you're a winner because you are exploring new ways to find happiness. And with each exploration, a world of possibilities can be found.

Even though Internet dating has been around for a while, I say 'new' because compared to the old way of dating, it's not even in its infancy yet. New things take time to grasp. Many experts believe it wasn't until 5000 BC that The Wheel was invented. Probably a lot of people said it would never work. Not probably—they did because it took another 500 years after its invention to be used. (I'm constantly amazed how many great inventions, ideas, books, movies, etc. started out as a struggle because so many people said, 'that's stupid' and/or 'no!' Imagine the number of great ideas that are sitting in a drawer because the person who invented it heard 'no' too often and gave up. NEVER give up if you believe in something. But, that's another book.)

Internet dating isn't nearly as important as the wheel, but it can set wheels in motion. Corny, but you get my point. Internet dating can help you achieve your goal. So why not be a fisherwoman, put on your Spider-Woman gear and hit the net?

Internet dating can speed up the process as well as introduce you to people you'd have never met because they aren't in the same line of work, they don't go to the same places you do, they don't know any of your friends, or they don't live in the area.

Yes, men will lie about some—many of the things they say about themselves: "I'm about 6'2" and people tell me I look like Brad Pitt" can end up meaning he's 5'4" and he looks more like an avocado pit. Remember, he's in the auditioning stage. Same goes for the kind of money he makes, car he drives, books he reads, museums he visits, deep, sensitive guy he is… he's auditioning for the job. In this case, he is actually writing out a resume in the form of a profile.

For the life of me, I don't understand why people blatantly lie on their profiles, considering if you like what you read and see, the reason you are meeting that person is you liked what you read and saw. This is where a cup of coffee can be much more satisfying than an entire meal. You can leave much faster if the guy's picture was taken in 2002 and he's changed. A lot.

Please remember what I said about guys saying they want to get married. He might have checked that off as a 'yes' on the list simply because he knows that's what many women want to hear. It may be true but he's not saying it about you. He hasn't even met you yet.

Writing a resume (profile) is easier than speaking it for many people, thus, another reason Internet dating is a good way to meet someone. If you're shy, you can be less so in writing. You can let your fingers do the talking and wait to see if anyone is listening.

One of my sisters is very shy, works all the time and is single. She didn't date for a long time. It took me and my two other sisters about two years to convince her to try Internet dating. Two years! We didn't tell her she had to do it for the rest of her life, we said, "just try it; what do you have to lose—except some loneliness." She finally acquiesced. She is now in a fantastic relationship with a guy she loves and loves her. Because she was finally open to new possibilities it led to a probability. Your life is like a circle. Inside it's all safe and you are comfortable. Outside not so much. Anytime you go outside—you expand your circle, thus expanding your probabilities and your life. Go past your comfort zone. Safely and smartly but do it. Most people never look back regretting the things they did. They regret what they didn't do).

Your profile will be the first thing a man sees about you and the first time he sees you. So, look your best. Make sure he can actually see what you look like and it's not all fuzzy—unless fuzzy is how you look in real life.

Don't use an old picture unless you really do still look like that. Remember, if you guys click you're going to meet. You don't want to see disappointment on his face when you walk into the room. That can be hurtful, and you are just wasting your time when it can be better spent.

Put in a picture that best represents what you look like and who you are. I say, "Who you are" because if you have an activity you love, put a picture in of you doing that. I have noticed that no matter what a person looks like, when they are doing something they love, they radiate something that is magical, and it translates to the viewer.

Don't just take a picture of you smiling, or looking sexy, by the way. You need *to feel it emotionally.* So have a reason you're smiling or feeling sexy. A great way to do that is to either think of something that puts you into that happy or sexy place, or the use of music, or both.

Don't put in pictures that aren't as good as the others. People will do this just to have more pictures. Less is more.

Speaking of which, *when you write out your profile, less is much, MUCH more.* Guys are going to: (1) See if they like what you look like. If they do, they are going to (2) Read what you have to say. If it's too long, they are going to (3) Tune out if you have too much to say. (I talk about this in an upcoming chapter.) Sure, they might still contact you because they liked the way you looked, but why not show him you can speak his language from the very moment you meet. You gain an advantage. You score points.

Start conditioning him to see you are the kind of woman he wants in his life.

Perhaps use a sports metaphor in your short profile, "I'm like the Super Bowl. Even during the commercials, I'm fun."

You'll be speaking his language.

Or use a movie quote: "I want a man who has me at hello."

A guy will read a movie quote and get it right away, sometimes even if it's a 'chick-flick' movie quote. We knuckle-draggers love movie quotes. LOVE them. Why? Because they are easy to understand. We've seen the movie and the context is right there.

Also, try to be a little unique. Look at your competition and see what they are writing. Usually a lot of the same stuff. Try to add a bit of flair to what you say. Something that will catch his attention. Even better, something that will make him smile. Even better still, something that will make him laugh. And best, something that isn't too long. That itself will be unique!

Once you start Internet dating, you might have to drink coffee with a lot of toads before you find that prince. But it's worth the shot.

I would *STRONGLY* suggest you meet for coffee the first time you meet. Meaning, I don't care how well you think you know this guy from emails, tweets, texts, Facebook, Instagram, Snapchat and phone calls, you don't know this guy. More than likely, he's not Hannibal Lector, but why risk being the meal when having one (coffee in this case) is such a better option.

Don't have him pick you up or you pick him up. Meet in a public place. That you feel safe in. (Can you tell I grew up with three sisters and my mom and I feel the need to protect?)

Also, beware of men who use the dating site as a 'hop into bed' site. Guys who are just looking for action will use dating sites for action. How can you tell if he's this guy? Yep, you got it. You watch his patterns. And you don't sleep with him right away. (I'll get to this in more detail in a bit.)

Why not take that small step to your computer, put down $20 to $40 bucks a month to try an Internet dating site for six months, and shoot your web wider than you could on your own? You and your happiness are well worth that time and money investment.

POINT VALUE: Infinite if it works and you get a man.

FOR THE SIX MEN READING THIS BOOK: Don't contact every woman you see and have no follow through. If you like what you see and what you read, then be sincere and make plans to meet. Use pictures from this century, even if you had hair in the last. And don't say you want to get married if you don't mean it. Then you're just a dick.

There's a Reason Some Sayings Stay Around Forever

A Man Loves It When a Woman Cooks for Him

"A good cook is like a sorceress who dispenses happiness."
— Elsa Schiaparelli
(Fused Surrealist Art with fashion)

A great way to reel in a man is with food. We've all heard the expression, "The fastest way to a man's heart is through his stomach." It's true. That's why that saying has been around forever. Why? We men LOVE eating a home-cooked meal. Now, some of you are saying, "That's obvious, but kiss my butt, Mr. Knuckle-dragger; I'm way too busy to cook."

You can "kiss my butt" all you want (uh, that didn't come out right), or you can come up with a new theory for "The shortest distance between two points is a straight line." Good luck, no one's been able to break that theory thus far.

Why not take the direct path?

This is such a big deal for so many men because from the very moment we were conceived, you fed us and housed us. Terrific womb service, by the way. Better than the Peninsula Hotel. Elven stars. Thank you. After we were evicted from our womb, without a 30-day notice or any kind of warning, I might add, we still needed to be fed so we would survive. Even after we got off the tit, many of our mothers still fed us by cooking for us.

Some of you ladies are saying, "Uh, Mr. Knuckle-dragger, there is such a thing as a baby girl. She was also fed, housed, and nurtured by a woman." True. So why isn't the saying, "The best way to a woman's heart is through her stomach?" Because for some reason, this is more appreciated by us men. Yes, you ladies love it when a man takes the time to cook you a meal. I have fun when I do it for a woman, and she usually appreciates it. But, I would score more points with you ladies in other areas. This is one where you score major points with men.

I think the reason this is more important to men than it is to women is because women are born instinctively knowing that they are going to be the child bearers, the ones who incubate and feed the baby so she/he can survive.

The home-cooked meal is a lost art. Like any treasure that has been lost, it is cherished when found. Most single men, and many men in relationships and marriages eat poorly or quickly or both. Restaurant dining, fast food gulping, supermarket sushi, packaged salad, or pre-heated rotisserie chicken, microwaved this, that and the other thing. This is a single man's routine like eight days a week. I'm not saying that women don't have the same issue when it comes to eating. But the reason you're reading this book is to learn things you can do to get what you want from a man; thus, I focus on what you can do to get a man. If you don't know how to cook, why not learn? Even if it's just one thing, learn to cook it in many different ways. If your man catches on, tell him you know how much he loves whatever the one thing is you cook, so that's why you always cook it for him. We're simple. We'll buy it. And even if he doesn't he will appreciate the effort.

I have a friend, Andy. Andy dated Maria. Andy said Maria was a great cook. It took him about six months to realize that she only made one thing; chicken. Lemon Pepper Chicken, boiled chicken, breaded chicken. It was all about the chicken. But it was damn good chicken. Andy and Maria eventually got married. Sure, her chicken cooking wasn't the only reason he married her—I think... but it scored her big points.

I know, if you have a job, kids to take care of, or both, it's hard to find the time. Find the time. Remember, we think you're Superwoman and we want you to be a Jeannie. I'm not saying to cook all the time. Most men are so starved for a home-cooked meal, once a month would be a blessing. Once a week—a Godsend. Remember, the more you do it, the more of a habit you become. (That being said, don't do it all the time. You want to change it up, so when you do it, it's special. That's true for just about everything in life.)

After the meal, he'll be as happy as a baby who has just been fed and burped. That's when you 'slaughter the lamb'.

When I was going out with Maggie, she would cook matzo brie every now and then. She made amazing matzo brie. I wasn't even a fan of it until she made it for me. (For those that don't know it's a breakfast dish usually made during Passover but can be made anytime. I have since tried to duplicate Maggie's matzo brie and not come close.) Whenever I would eat her brie, I was in heaven. (Ladies— minds out of the gutter please.) I think she made it whenever she felt I was about to end our rocky relationship—and whenever she'd make it, I'd think as I was shoveling bites into my mouth, "Sure she's neurotic, clingy, incredibly insecure, materialistic, argumentative and downright mean to just about everyone... but maybe it can work!"

Now, if that's running through my head with that kind of relationship, imagine what cooking can do for a healthy relationship, a relationship where you've scored many points, but he's still on the fence. Cooking is one of those things that can get him off the fence and onto one knee.

Make him a scrumptious meal every now and then. While he's putting the food into his belly, put into his mind thoughts of the two of you being together. He's full. He's happy. More importantly, he's vulnerable. His defenses are down, and his mind and heart are open. DON'T pressure cook. He'll run so fast, he'll make The Road Runner look like a tortoise. Simply plant the seed.

Subtly, like a whisper.

POINT VALUE: + 9.999999

FOR THE SIX MEN READING THIS BOOK: Any woman who is willing to take time out of her busy schedule to cook for you is not only a Jeannie, she's a GODDESS. Treat her like one. Show her how much you appreciate what she's doing. Bring her flowers. Write her a poem. Dance with her in the living room. Tell her how much you love her and how beautiful she is. You'll score points. Sometimes, you can even bank these points for a later time when you want to do something. As she can bank points for all the great stuff she does for you.

The Promised Land

Protect Your Heart. Don't Sleep with Him Right
Away

*"If all the girls who attended the Yale prom were laid
end to end, I wouldn't be a bit surprised."*
– Dorothy Parker
(One of American's and the world's greatest satirists)

WHENEVER I give advice to my sisters, or female friends on the subject of relationships, my number one goal, bar none, is to protect their hearts. Thus, the reason I am about to write what I'm about to write.

Sex is our strongest instinct. Procreation = survival. Thus, the reason we all want to have sex and the reason that it's so enjoyable. Well, if done correctly and for more than 30 seconds. If sex felt like sticking pins all over your body, the human race would have died out... oh, about 15 days after its birth.

With men, when it comes to sex and a woman we want, we are relentless. We become Sméagol turning into Gollum from Lord of the Rings.

"I must have the precious!" In order to get to the Promised Land, many guys will say what they think you want to hear and/or be what they think you want them to be. They will put up a show that would make the greatest Las Vegas act envious. Remember, they are auditioning.

Once many guys get 'the precious', things can change. For a multitude of reasons:

1   Biologically, we've planted our seed to procreate (survive); time to move on and plant more seeds!

2   We men love to conquer, and we conquered that particular 'territory', so once again, it's time to move on. In this case, to climb a new 'Everest'.

3   Some men are looking for that perfect sex partner. Even though perfection does not exist, he will still try and find it. These are men usually in the Ungettable column.

Numbers one, two, and three can happen because the guy had no real time to know you as a person and still regarded you as an object. This next reason, number four, is the one I want to focus on.

1   Emotions are all confused, and we realize what we thought was love was just lust, so we move on.

2   Yes, surprisingly, sex can affect men in an emotional way too. (Many men won't ever admit this.) However, sex can also mean absolutely nothing emotionally. (Most men will certainly claim this.)

How can you tell what he's after? What he really wants? YOU WAIT.

NOTE: Not only do the six men reading this book hate me right now, as well as many of you ladies, but every single person who knows me is thinking; "Did jD just say wait? Was he drugged when he said this?" With all due respect to my friends, I was not drugged. Yes, I love sex, but I know it can really confuse the situation and lead to you getting hurt much more so than if sex had not entered the equation.

Would I say to a woman I was on a date with, "I really want to have sex with you, but I want to wait until we get to know each other?"

No. I don't know many guys who would. And the guys who do say it are usually using it as a ploy to get the woman into bed. Thus, the reason I tell you this here and now because chances are when I'm sitting across from you and the evening has gone well, I'm not going to suggest we wait. Mini Me would have me committed.

See that was Mini Me talking and he does a lot of talking and thinking for us men when it comes to sex! He wants to boldly jump in right away, without any long-term regards for your feelings or the feelings of the man he owns.

I'm NOT telling you to wait because if you have sex with a man too fast he won't respect you. This kind of man is called 'Asshole Face'. Yes, I know there is a double standard when it comes to sex, but if I'm not mistaken, Mr. Asshole Face didn't wait either, so who is he to judge? In my opinion, this kind of man has a steamer trunk full of issues and why bother with him at all because those issues will eventually surface. I am telling you to wait because I want you to protect your heart.

Carl Jung said, "The meeting of two personalities is like the contact of two chemical substances: if there is any reaction, both are transformed."

IF there is any reaction... because that's not always the case. If there is a reaction, is it a real one or one that has been manufactured by hopeful thinking?

The longer you wait, the better chance that feeling of true love is not manufactured. You have a better understanding of him and whether or not you believe he and you will both be 'transformed'.

In sports, the best offense is a great defense. Offense sells tickets, defense wins games. In your case, your offense is you; you sold the ticket and got him to the game. Now you use your defense to protect your heart, so if it doesn't work out, you haven't lost the game. You've won because you're able to move on to the next game with fewer injuries.

How long you wait or even if you wait is your individual choice.

I am, however, strongly suggesting that you don't jump into bed and have intercourse with a guy after the first date, or the second, or the third, or the forth, or even the fifth. (Mini Me is incredibly upset with me right now.) Give the relationship time to develop. That way, you'll get to know the man without the many confusing emotional attachments that come with sex. Intercourse runs deeper than any other sex act there is... emotionally. Kissing and intercourse go directly to the heart. When two people are kissing, they are truly one. When a man's inside a woman, they are totally one. There is a reason why that act and that act alone is called 'making love'.

I'm not saying you need to wait on everything. As far as other sexual activities go, that all depends on how much they mean to you *emotionally*. A grunter can slide into second and third base without it affecting the heart the same way intercourse does. (Isn't it interesting how, once again, a sports term is used when we men grunt about sex?) Same is true for oral sex, which for some reason has no 'base' designated to it and is perhaps the reason why many people, including a former president, do not consider a blowjob a sexual act. Of course, it is. But for us guys, it would help to have a base designated to it so we would know for sure.

We've all become numb about having sex, but our hearts haven't, so sex confuses us. It's so easy to get, it has become like Starbucks. There's one on every corner. Sometimes, two right across the street from each other!

Imagine if there was only one Starbucks in the world, it was difficult to get to; and the first time you went there, they didn't serve you. They made you wait. Imagine how special that coffee would taste and how much you'd learn about that coffee while you waited. You might decide you don't want that particular type of coffee and move on without doing nearly as much damage to your wallet had you had that coffee.

Same holds true for relationships. Imagine how strong and sustaining a relationship you could have if, before sex came into the mix, you got to know one another.

Many studies have shown that love and being in love are fueled by chemicals and *chemistry* within our brains and that sex increases those chemicals.

Ever hear someone say, "We have chemistry?" Or "Yeah, I really liked him/her. They were great looking, fun, funny, smart, kind… but there just wasn't any chemistry between us?" Here's why:

When two people are attracted to each other, a virtual explosion of adrenaline-like neurochemicals gush forth. Fireworks explode and they see stars. Phenylethylamine (PEA) is a chemical that speeds up the flow of information between nerve cells. Also involved are dopamine and norepinephrine, chemical cousins of amphetamines.

Dopamine makes us feel good and norepinephrine stimulates the production of adrenaline. It makes our heart race, our hands sweat, and our blood flow. These things happen inside of us chemically; it's naturally produced in our bodies, so we survive. When fireworks explode and we see stars, we want to mate. Thus, the reason sex can confuse the issue. Acting upon these chemical stimulants can make us feel or think we are in love when in fact we are only in heat.

The bad news is, no matter how much you might like him or he might like you, if that chemistry doesn't exist, no book, no course, nothing can make that into a passionate, loving, lasting relationship. You might try, you might try very hard because there is SOOOOO much greatness to this person and on that yellow pad they have one thousand reasons why on the "Plus" side and only one reason on the "Negative" side, that reason being "No chemistry", so your best bet is to stop trying to force that square peg into the round hole and become friends. As you know, there's nothing wrong with having a lasting, loving relationship with a friend.

The good news about chemistry is that when the infatuation subsides, a new group of chemicals takes over. This new type of chemical is created by endorphins. These morphine-like opiates calm and reassure us with intimacy, dependability, warmth, and shared experiences. Not as exciting or as stressful as PEA, but steadier and more addictive, leading to a healthy and longer-lasting relationship and even a longer life.

Studies show that chocolate can give you the same kind of high and satisfaction as sex. Thus, further proving my point that, when it comes to relationships and learning how to get a man, *practical experience* is much better and far more superior than scientific studies. Yes, sure, chocolate can give you a temporary high and make you feel better when you're depressed. That's because it's full of phenylethylamine, a chemical cousin of amphetamines.

But I have never ever heard any man or woman say, "I was so horny and really wanted to get some action, but thank The Universe for that chocolate bar because I now realize I can get that feeling whenever I want for only a buck 50! Yeeessssss!!!" I've never tried to fuck a chocolate bar but I'm pretty sure it's not as good as being with a woman, and, although I am not a woman, even though most men are clueless in bed, I'd like to believe most men fuck better than a Snickers Bar. Perhaps you're snickering because I'm wrong. Okay, maybe. But try to cuddle with the Snickers Bar and see how that goes. Ha! One point for men. Even though we don't like cuddling and suck at it.

Unless ol' Willy and his Wonker pops out of the chocolate bar, chocolate is not going to do the trick.

You might be thinking, "Okay, Mr. Knuckle-dragger, maybe I'll wait, but I've been fantasizing about this guy and my sex drive is just as strong as any man's. Maybe, even stronger. What do you expect me to do?" Why not enjoy the foreplay[4] for the time being?

Then, when you finally let him in, you will—wait! What am I talking about? You're dating a man. His idea of foreplay is the drive over. Okay, here's what you do. You ladies know that there are plenty of products on the market that can stimulate you and satisfy some of your sexual needs—better than a lot of men. Buy one. Use it. True, you can't cuddle with the rabbit, thank The Universe, because the survival of the

---

[4] This is for you men, because I know, you ladies know what foreplay is: dinner and a movie. Okay, okay, I jest. It's just dinner. Men, brothers, fellow toads—you don't have to charge the castle the moment the gate comes down. She has lips, a neck, ears, shoulders, stomach, inner thighs, outer thighs… I know you know about the breasts, but a juggle and a pull don't cut it. Then, there's that area called 'Heaven'. There's nothing like a taste of Heaven. Just be prepared to taste for a while if you want Heaven to be happy. I've got it! A way you can understand foreplay. Think of her body like baseball. If you hit a home run and just stood there and touched the plate, you wouldn't get to feel the glory building up as you round the bases. It's much more fun to go to FIRST base first. You get to see the joy and excitement on fan's faces. You relish in it as you head to SECOND. It builds up even more as you go to THIRD. You can feel your fans about to explode and as you slide into HOME, she screams in ecstasy! I mean your fans scream with joy. Everyone congratulates you. You're a hero. A superhero! You're the man! Be that man with her. Be a superhero in bed.

human race would be in jeopardy. But, it sure can get you off. So, I've been told. Many times. By many different women. Hey, are they trying to tell me something?

A by-product of waiting is: he might actually learn what foreplay is because it's all he'll be getting for a while. If you ever decide to let him get to heaven, he's been trained. He has formed a habit. He might actually take some time to get there and not just rush past 'Go'. Triple/Double/Quadruple!

If the guy you're dating is not willing to stick around because he's not getting any, you should really ask yourself, "Self, is this a man I really want to be with?" "Why can't he wait?" "What does he really want from me?"
Let's say, you've now spent some time with him and you have not had sex. You won't see things through those "he's great in bed" rose-colored glasses because you didn't let him in. Literally. You'll have a clearer view.

***

Let's say your view is you like him and care about him, but realize he really isn't the guy you want to spend the rest of your life with. It will be so much easier for you to end it because as much as you care about him—you'd care more if you had slept with him—even though he's the same guy who you've come to realize you don't want. (Unless of course he is sooooo bad in bed. Then you might not care at all when it ends).

Let's say you've dated him for a while and you really think he's the one, but he ends up walking away from you. Yes, it's going to hurt, but again, not nearly as much as if you slept with him. At least, this is what I've experienced from women who have told me they got hurt by a guy.

That's how powerful sex is! It makes you feel things that aren't necessarily real.

My friend Sally recently asked for my advice about dating. She's in her early forties, been divorced for two years, and has a six-year-old. During the conversation, she mentioned a guy who she had dated and really cared about. Let's call him Ed. Then she talked about another guy she

107

dated, I don't remember for sure, but I think she said his name was Loser.

Mr. Loser had problems because Sally has a kid, and, for whatever reason, this pushed a button in him.

Sally said that he worked all the time, never really had time for her, and named several other flaws in his personality. Yet, it really hurt when he broke it off with her. She misses him and thinks about calling him often. Ed, who was a great guy, fun to be with, liked her kid and seemed to have no red flag flaws, broke it off with her, and she doesn't miss him. She said it hurt at first, but not for long.

"Sometimes, it just doesn't work out," was what she said to me about Ed. Then, she pined about Mr. Loser and wanted to know if she should call him and try to go back with him. Guess what? Yep, you got it. She never slept with Ed, but she had slept with Mr. Loser.

Do what you can to hold your heart—I mean vajaja—in check. That way you can see if this guy really wants to be with you and more importantly *if you really want to be with him.* Remember what they used to say about giving away the milk. Milk might have an expiration date—sex does not.

POINT VALUE: Infinite amount of points for yourself if it doesn't work out and you've waited. When it ends, it won't hurt nearly as much. Infinite amount of points if it does work out because you've waited and gotten to know each other and realize that there is much you have outside the bedroom.

FOR THE SIX MEN READING THIS BOOK: Sorry about this chapter. By the way, your woman wants it as bad as you do. She's not doing it to punish you, she's doing it to get to know you and you have to respect that. Sure, it will be frustrating, but that's why you have long enough arms to scratch that itch.

NOTE: You not only want to protect your heart, but you also need to protect your body. What and if you use birth control is your choice. Most people know about getting checked for AIDS and Herpes. But many don't know about an STD called Human Papilloma Virus (HPV). It can lead to cervical cancer. So, get checked if you are going to be sexually active. Make sure the term 'loaded gun' is just that, a term—and not the real thing.

Work out the Kinks

Sexual Compatibility is Very Important

"My toughest fight was with my first wife."
— Muhammad Ali
(Boxer, Trailblazer, World Changer)

NO matter how much we try to deny or suppress it, no matter how many taboos are placed on it, no matter what you were taught or what was 'beaten' out of you, we are sexual beings.

Some people are more sexual than others. If you're one of those in the 'more sexual' category, you're going to need a man who is in that category as well. And those in that category have a list of things they like and don't like, they've tried and never want to do again, they haven't tried and want someone to try it with. Whatever 'it' is.

As long as 'it' is between two (or more) ***CONSENTING ADULTS***—and *no one else or nothing else will get hurt*—whatever 'it' is, is your prerogative.

You and your man should have a similar 'kink' factor. You should be compatible with each other's wants and desires in bed—or on dining-room floors, elevators, kitchen tables, and/or chandeliers.

Once you've waited and are ready to go the distance with your man (and of course, you've waited), you are going to learn things he likes and doesn't like sexually; just as he's going to learn these things about you.

In some relationships, you learn them together. Sometimes you'll learn with him what you do like and didn't realize you liked. Those are amazing times.

If he's into 'this' and 'this' is important to him, but you're not into 'this', he might look elsewhere for 'this'. Same goes for your 'this', 'that', and the other 'thing', that's important to you. You can't argue or fight over what you like and he doesn't or vice versa. It is what it is, and you have to accept it. Or move on. Remember, you want to close a door so you can open a new one. There's no reason to stay with a man who's not giving what you desire sexually if what you desire sexually is important to you.

If he's Mr. Gotta Get Some all the time and you're not, there's a good chance he's going to look for it elsewhere. If you're a sexual dynamo, but he'd rather play Wolfenstein II: The New Colossus, there's a good chance you're going to get frustrated and want to play with someone else. Like I said, The Rabbit is a great temporary substitute, but it can't cuddle you, stroke your hair, and tell you how damn sexy you look.

"What are you talking about, Mr. Knuckle-dragger? My man doesn't do any of that AND he snores!"

POINT VALUE: Plus ten if you both like 'this', 'that', and that 'other thing'—whatever 'this', 'that', and that 'other thing' might be. Minus ten if sex is really important to you or him and if he (or you) like something that is important for your sexual fulfillment and you (or he) doesn't.

FOR THE SIX MEN READING THIS BOOK: Same holds true for all of you, Knuckle-draggers. Many of you think sex isn't as important to a woman as it is to a man. Many of you are idiots. So if you're not into scratching her itch, she will seek someone who is.

Dental Floss or Burka?

Make Sure He's Comfortable with What You Wear

"A man cannot be comfortable without his own approval."
– Mark Twain
(One of the greatest American writers and satirists)

IT'S up to you what bait you want to wear when you're out on the hunt, but don't forget what they say about "first impressions". Many guys will hit on a woman who dresses like Kim K. Many guys will want them to dress like soon to be princess Markle once they are dating.

Let's say your man is the kind who loves when you dress really sexy because he loves to show you off—makes him feel like the King Knuckle-dragger. He loves that other knuckle-draggers look at him and grunt, "How does he do it?" If you're cool with that, great. Dress less. Let's say you're not comfortable dressing like this for one or more reasons. Maybe you don't want to be considered a trophy. Maybe you don't feel safe dressing that way because you know what other men are thinking and you don't want them to get the wrong idea.

Whatever your reasons, you are entitled to them and you should be honest with him. Perhaps say something like, "Honey, I really don't want to do the dental floss thing. I'm with you—I don't need bait to land another fish." If your guy can't understand that and insists—perhaps it's time to find one who is a little more secure.

What if your man is uncomfortable with how you dress? What if he isn't into you wearing three pieces of lint? You can tell him to piss off, this is how you dressed when you met, and he has no business telling you how to dress. Or, you could put yourself in your man's shoes and try to see why he might not be comfortable with something you wear. If you don't care why, why are you with this guy? Sure, if you feel you need to give him a wake-up call, go for it. But when things are going good, he knows he has you there is no reason for you to lose points by doing something that makes him ill at ease.

Why would he be uncomfortable? Perhaps he's worried that you're still on the hunt because you're still wearing bait and looking to catch a better fish. Maybe he hates it when guys stare at you because he knows what they are thinking, and he doesn't like it. Maybe your guy is worried it's not safe for you (Please don't get me wrong with what I just said. Doesn't matter what a woman is wearing or not wearing. If a woman is walking down the street completely naked singing Lil' Kim's "How Many Licks" after she just had sex w/10 guys and wants #11. Number 11 doesn't mean you. NO MAN HAS THE RIGHT TO TOUCH ANY WOMAN UNLESS AND UNTIL SHE CONSENTS!!! PERIOD! To those men who can't handle a woman dressing "too sexy" make sure you are restrained from head-to-toe whenever you're around women. Otherwise don't ever be around women. Or cut off your Mr. Can't Be Controlled so hopefully your sick power trip will be cut off as well. Rape and Abuse are done by little non-human, non-man feeling big by making a woman feel small or maybe your man is worried that he could get into a fight.

I was at a bar with my friend Ted, who saw a woman sitting by herself, wearing bait and not much of it. Ted went over and introduced himself. He talked to her for about eight seconds when suddenly this guy comes up behind him and gets in his face. Mr. Bruised Ego tells Ted that she's with him. It turns out Mr. Bruised Ego was in the bathroom and now wants to fight Ted—which is a big mistake because Ted is the kind of guy you never want to get into a fight with. Luckily, Ted walked away.

What did Ted say to me, his fellow grunter? "Jakey, if she hadn't been wearing that 'fuck me' outfit, I wouldn't have hit on her."

Whatever your man's reasons for being uncomfortable, why do anything to encourage another man to hit on you and discourage your man from getting down on one knee for you?

Does this sound a bit old-fashioned? Yes. Am I saying you should dress like a spinster or from head-to-toe in a burka? No. Should you look and feel sexy when you want to? Absolutely! Should you look like a billboard for Ho's Ville? If he doesn't like it I would suggest not.

I told my friend Danellia that she always dressed sexy, but not in a "are you a hooker?" kind of way. She said the trick was to have one-piece sexy, either the top or bottom and the other more conservative.

Is it really that important to put some thin lines of thread between you and your man? You dress a certain way for work. You "dress for success." Don't you consider getting a man a success?

Yes, getting attention is great. But isn't it better to protect your man's feelings if he doesn't like you dressed to undress and win points than getting attention from a bunch of horny dawgs, who are looking for nothing more than a place to bury their bone for the evening?

SUBCONSCIOUS POINT VALUE: Plus three for dressing a way that makes both you and him happy and comfortable. Minus six for making him uncomfortable.

FOR THE SIX MEN READING THIS BOOK: Guess what, dumbass? If she needs to get attention from strangers, she's not getting it from you.

Paper or Plastic?

Lingerie, Old T-Shirt, Whatever. Find Out What
He Considers Sexy in Bed and Wear It.

*"So I'm licking jelly off my boyfriend and all of a sudden I'm
thinking 'Oh God, I'm turning into my mother'."*
— Sarah Silverman
(Comedian, actor, fearless trailblazer)

YOU'VE heard it, I'll repeat it: "Many men want their woman to be a whore in the bedroom and Madonna out of it." Is that fair? No. Is it the way men think? Yes.

The way you dress when you're in public is one thing, how you dress for bed is another matter. So why not find out what type of clothing turns on the man you want when it comes to sex? Of course, you've waited a long enough for this step because first, you want to get to know him and make sure you're not wasting your time, right? Right.

If you are comfortable with what he likes you to wear, go for it. Some guys like sexy lingerie.

Some guys like cheerleader outfits.

Silk PJs

An undershirt

Any of his shirts

A football, basketball, whatever jersey

Heels

Handcuffs

Boots

Various costumes

Newspaper

Money

Tinfoil

Bunny ears

Paper bags

Plastic suits

Wigs (If you do this, don't get mad if he's hotter for you than he's been in a while. It's still you.)

Whatever 'it' is, and he probably has more than one 'it', find out what 'it' is and surprise him by wearing 'it'. Clothing can enhance your sexiness and heighten his anticipation. One of the 'its' that turn me on is a Santa Hat. Don't really know why. Maybe it's because being with a woman is like Christmas morning and I love to get that wrapping paper off and then see the present inside.

Ask your man what he finds sexy for you to wear in bed. By asking, you score points for not only wearing it but for being concerned enough about his wants and desires. Another benefit is you might have your way with him more often. Triple/Double!

Do not wear 'it' all the time. You don't want it to become too familiar because then it can lose its appeal. Which brings me to another suggestion, when it comes to what to wear, or not to wear. Don't walk around naked all the time. I'm not a prude. I just feel that clothing helps keep the mystery going— even after he has seen you naked a billion times. It's still more fun to have to peel off layers to get to you. Like a present, it's more fun to open it up when it's a gift wrapped than have someone toss it to you with a "here's your new computer." Sure, you still love the computer—but you lose that moment of mystery and the excitement that comes along with it. We like 'mystery' even if we know what's underneath the wrapping. There are even times when it's a great surprise to see more wrapping under the wrapping.

There's a reason a strip club is not called a 'Naked Club'. There's a reason why women who perform at these clubs are called strippers and not 'nakeders'. Coming on stage already naked is not as thrilling as watching her strip off clothing.

Find out what's sexy to him. He'll love it and you'll love the results because you'll score BONEness points. (I couldn't resist).

POINT VALUE: Plus three

FOR THE SIX MEN READING THIS BOOK: Many women love role-play. Find out what she likes. Maybe she's always wanted to have sex with a fireman (seems a lot of women do), or a hockey player, Roman gladiator, police officer, famous writer (Yeah, that's WAY up there ☺ Whatever it is, go for it. She gets her fantasy and you get to shoot off your gun.

Put Your Money Where Your Mouth Is

Men Love Blowjobs!

"If I could find a way to have sex with myself that was as exciting as it is with a woman, I'd live in a white tower and never come out."

– Rod Steiger

(Academy Award-winning actor, married five times, Go figure)

MEN love blowjobs!

That will conclude this chapter.

Turn Your Bathroom into a Magazine Stand

> Men Like Something to Read While They're in the Bathroom

"I suggest that the only books that influence us are those for which we are ready and which have gone a little further down our particular path than we have yet gone ourselves."

– E.M. Forster

(English author. Great works include, 'Howards End' and 'Room with a View')

YOU might be thinking, "A supplementary income is nice, but I really don't want to sell magazines, gum and candy out of my bathroom, Mr. Knuckle-dragger."

Why not, you never know who you'll meet? Okay, your bathroom is not a good way to meet anyone... but it is a great way to get someone you already met. I need to explain. Men have many needs, and sometimes they are, uh, quirky. One of those quirky needs is that we men like to read in the bathroom.

You might now be thinking, "Mr. Knuckle-dragger, why on earth would you designate an entire chapter to this subject? Why not just put it in some other chapter, like "Stuff to Do in Your Home" or "Men Want the Stupidest Things"?

Two reasons why. One: you already know. Even the smallest of advantages can lead you to victory and yes, this is a small one.

Two: if you wanted to fly a plane, it would be a very good idea to have everything on board you need to ensure a smooth take-off, ride and landing *before* you stepped into the cockpit. (Also important to understand all you can about that plan like reading this MANual. I mean a plan manual). That includes things you might need and/or hope you don't need. You want to be 110% prepared.

By the way, the plane's brain center is the 'cockpit'. The man's brain center is in his... Yeah, you got it. Very interesting.

Anyway, why not do everything you can to ensure a smooth take-off, great landing, and long ride with the man you want to take on this journey?

When he uses your bathroom, he'll read whatever is nearby. So, put in magazines *you* want him to read.

You know, stuff about relationships and how a man should treat a woman. He'll never realize you did that for your benefit (and his). He'll just think those are the magazines and/or articles you keep for you. Triple/Double. You might be the first person in history who, after he announces he has to go to the bathroom says, 'Take your time'.

Let's face facts: if libraries were in men's bathrooms, men would be much more informed.

Why do we men like our reading in the bathroom? Many reasons. One of them is we have a very good chance of not being bothered in there by anyone. For many men, it's a sanctuary. It's our Bat Cave. I understand this to be ten-fold for men who are married, and a thousand-fold when they are married with children. It's one of the only places in the house a man, especially one with kids, can find quiet time.

This is so important to men that I know one guy who built his bathroom into such a Bat Cave that he could practically live in it. He had a flat screen TV, shelves for books, magazines, and newspapers, a little desk for his laptop and a refrigerator stocked with beer.

Other men would go to his house, see his Bat Cave masterpiece, and weep with envy. Okay, they wouldn't weep in front of other knuckle-draggers. But they sure did wish they could have a bathroom like his!

I'm not saying you need to go to this extreme and build out your bathroom. However, I am strongly suggesting you go that little extra mile and put magazines and/or books in the bathroom. Little things like this become a runway of possibilities.

SUBCONSCIOUS POINT VALUE: Plus one. However, this is worth more points for you personally if you choose magazines and/or books that contain articles you want him to read.

FOR THE SIX MEN READING THIS BOOK: For the sake of all those innocent people inside the house, please, PLEASE spray some air freshener when you're done!

There's No Crying in Baseball!

If You're Going to Use Tears to Manipulate Him, Make Sure You Pick Your Battles in Order to Win the War

"There is always some madness in love. But, there is also always some reason in madness."

— Friedrich Nietzsche
(Late 19th century German philosopher)

I'M not talking about real honest-to-goodness reasons to cry tears. I'm talking about the ones used to manipulate the situation to your advantage. "All's fair in love and war," but if you're going to use those tears, save them for the important things, things that will win you the war, not just the battle. If you pull this ploy too much, too often, about too many things—your man is going to think of you as an emotional terrorist or an emotional wreck and either way you'll lose points.

SUBCONSCIOUS POINT VALUE: Minus seven if you're consistently crying over spilled milk.

FOR THE SIX MEN READING THIS BOOK: Georgy Porgy, they aren't all fake. Did you ever stop to think that you might have said or done something that hurt her and made her cry? Read in between the lines. She's not crying 'cause the milk just spilled. She's crying for real reasons, perhaps because she's not getting the attention she used to get from you. Don't think it's always a manipulation. Something bad or sad might have happened. Don't be an idiot and grunt, "Are you PMSing?" every time your woman cries. Be a man, take her into your arms, and make her feel better.

Ready or Not, I'm Not

> Eight o'clock Doesn't Mean 9:45. Don't Make
> Him Wait for You. Be on Time.

*"I would like to say that the first time Adam had a chance,
he laid the blame on a woman."*
— Nancy Astor
(First woman to serve as a member of the British House of
Commons)

YOU know that frustrated look on your man's face when you say you'll be ready by 8:00 pm and at 8:15 pm, he's still waiting, now pacing, now checking his cell or watch for the hundredth time? Try to be ready when you say you'll be ready. He'll be shocked that you are on time because he has dated many women who aren't, and we men are very impatient creatures. We get all tight and frustrated inside for really no reason, but we do.

If you say you'll be ready at 8:00 pm, why not make believe you need to be ready by 7:45? Better yet, 6:15? That way, you're still going to be late, but not late, late.

POINT VALUE: Minus one if you always keep a man after you've agreed upon a time to go. Plus three subconscious points if you're on time, more often than not.

FOR THE SIX MEN READING THIS BOOK: Chances are no matter what you do, she's going to be late. We leave the seat up, make messes, make unreasonable demands, say insensitive things, say stupid things and expect more than a newborn infant... so, cut her some slack. Remember, she's getting ready for you! She wants to look good for you! If you want, tell her you need to be at the event at 7:00 pm, when it starts at 7:30 pm. If she's still late, tell her it's okay, that you understand. You'll score BIG points. By the way, want to score bigger points? If she is or isn't late, when you see her, tell her how great she looks and how lucky you are.

Ahhhhhhhhhh! Anything but That!!!

> Don't Ask Your Man to Hold Your Purse

"When a young lady is to be a heroine, the perverseness of forty surrounding families cannot prevent her. Something must and will happen to throw a hero in her way."

– Jane Austen

(Great English author. Wrote 'Sense and Sensibility', 'Pride and Prejudice')

SEND us into the jungle to fight lions. Give us groceries that weigh 3000 pounds. Ask us to get the wine in the cellar, even though it's flooded, and alligators now live down there. We'll do that. We're okay with that. What we don't want to do, ever, is hold your handbag, pocketbook, or purse.

We men have big egos. (I will get to why very shortly.) We don't look manly with a handbag. If some guy wants to start something for some reason, we don't want to hit him with your purse. If we were smart we would, 'cause whatever you have inside gives it enough weight to knock him out for a week.

I'm not really sure why this 'could you please hold my purse' thing happens. Most men don't understand why either. We've seen what you're capable of carrying. I once saw a woman carrying a purse while holding a baby, while dragging luggage, while drinking bottled water, while holding bags of groceries and once, also carrying an elephant—all at the same time. (Okay, I have yet to see a woman carry all this stuff and an elephant. But, why do I feel like one day I will?) I've seen women holding more stuff than ten men combined. So to this day, much like the taking off the bra under the shirt trick, it is

125

a mystery to me and to most men that you need us to hold your purse.

SUBCONSCIOUS POINT VALUE: Minus one if you're always leaving him holding the bag.

FOR THE SIX MEN READING THIS BOOK: I don't understand purse-holding and I hate purse-holding as much as you do. So, my only advice is to deal with it. Like I said earlier, your woman puts up with a lot of your crap. She's not jumping for joy when she has to pick up that pile of clothes. And that pile over there. And the one over there. And Oh Christ, throw out that pair of underwear already!

Mittens

Keep Your Pet Away When Wanting to Get
Intimate

*"Cats are intended to teach us that not everything in nature
has a function."*
— Unknown

LADIES, if you have a cat or dog, it's very disconcerting to
be making intimate moves on you and most certainly making
love with you, to look over and see mittens watching. We feel
like we're being judged. We feel like your cat or dog is going
to talk about our performance to other cats or dogs. Mainly,
we're worried that Mr. or Ms. Mittens is going to freak-out
and think our nuts are a scratch toy.

If you want your man to spend the night often, let Mittens spend the night in another room. Sure, Mittens might get a little ticked off, but you two can bond again in the morning and assure yourself many more evenings with the man you also want to bond with.

POINT VALUE: Minus two if you must snuggle waggle, smoogle woogle, kissy wissy. Mittens a million times before you tell her or him they can't stay in the bedroom—and then, change your mind.

FOR THE SIX MEN READING THIS BOOK: Most of us men know to put Sparky into another room when it comes time for getting down to business. Sparky might be our best friend, but he has no idea how to run a camera, so who needs him. If she doesn't realize that her pet out of the bedroom during intimacy is Man Protocol, ask her if it's okay that mittens spend the night in the living room.

If she says, "No, Mittens always likes to sleep on my head and it's a must no matter what," you might consider finding another woman to be gotten by.

Grunt Time

Give Your Man the Space He Asks for, or Eventually He Will Find His Own Space Far, Far Away from You

"Some things... arrive on their own mysterious hour, on their own terms and not yours, to be seized or relinquished forever."

– Gail Godwin
(Author. Among her best sellers, 'A Mother and Two Daughters' and 'The Finishing School')

WE men love our space, which I call 'Grunt Time'. Just like you ladies like your 'Girl Time'. I have found that most men understand 'Girl Time', but there seems to be a lot of women who aren't big fans of 'Grunt Time'.

Maybe, I'm 'all wet'[5] on this one, but I don't think so.

Ladies, your man is not always up to no-good. If you think he is, why are you with him? Without trust, there is no 'us'. Corny, but you get my point. Let your man have his space.

Say to your man, "Honey, if there are times you need your space, let me know, and I'm fine with it." We rarely, if ever, hear this from a woman and you will score major points because you understand that this is part of our nature. Again, why fight nature when you can use her to your advantage? Be a surfer and go with the flow. Ride your man-wave so you both end up having the ride of your lifetime... TOGETHER.

POINT VALUE: Plus eight if you give him grunt time. Minus seven if you consistently are upset that he wants grunt time.

---

[5] A term meaning, 'Maybe, I'm wrong' used in movies from the 30s and 40s that I think is cool and I want to bring back into the vernacular.

FOR THE SIX MEN READING THIS BOOK: There are times even though you want space, you should be sensitive to why she needs you there. During those times, be there for her. After all, she recently took the time to cook you that great meal and didn't get upset with you when you said you were going out with your buddies to the game.

Pull My Finger

Yes, Some of His Friends Are Idiots. But They
are His Idiot Friends. Learn to Deal with It

*"I always felt that the great high privilege, relief, and
comfort of friendship was that one had to explain nothing."*
— Katherine Mansfield
(One of New Zealand's greatest writers)

YEAH, your man's friend Larry enjoys pretending he's a
walrus by sticking pencils up his nose. Your pencils. Ones
you actually use. It doesn't help matters that your man laughs
when Larry does this. This is one of those, 'deal with it'
situations. A guy's buds are really important to him—just like
your friends are important to you. Why not like his friends—
or at least do your best to find something, anything you like
about Larry, even if it's the mere fact that at the end of the
day he goes home. Hopefully.

Larry and your man have been friends since they were six.
Be glad your man grew out of it. Well, hopefully, he did.
Sometimes even us good ones revert back to the times of
youthful 'imbecillism'.

Liking his friends can even be more important than liking
his family, because many men see, hang, and are more open
and honest with their friends than they are with their family.
That being said; like his family as well. They love to throw in
their two cents, so you might as well let them spend their
money to say, "She's a keeper!"

More than likely, however, it is his buddy's "two cents"
he will hear the most. They are his counsel when seeking
advice and he WILL seek advice and opinions about you from

them. You want them to like you. Otherwise, his friends become fierce opponents.

If you really can't stand his friends, use that to your advantage: "Honey, why don't you go to Larry's without me? I'm sure you two would like to spend some grunt time together."

You just gave him his space. You just told him to have grunt time. You just showed him you understand his needs, AND you got out of hanging with Larry the Walrus. Triple/Double.

SUBCONSCIOUS POINT VALUE: Plus six if you're cool about his friends. Minus eight if you give him grief about still being friends with these freakin' morons and are always telling your man what a bunch of freakin' morons his friends are.

FOR THE SIX MEN READING THIS BOOK: Not for nothing, but some of your friends are freakin' morons. Not many women want to hang with a bunch of grunters who still like to fart the alphabet. As far as both friends and family opinions go, YOU'RE the one dating her, not them. Go with your heart and your gut and make your own decision.

Remember what Voltaire said, "I can protect myself from my enemies. God save me from my friends."

Pick-Up Sticks

Don't Complain That He Leaves Piles of
Clothes Around the House

"You must do the things you think you cannot."
– Eleanor Roosevelt
(Champion of the underprivileged. She transformed the role
of First Lady from serving tea to dishing out political
wisdom.)

WHY fight and argue over things you know aren't going to
change and when you come down to it, aren't that big of a
deal?

Men are not going to pick up that pile of clothes on the
floor no matter how many times you ask, beg, or yell. Okay,
we might pick them up once in a while, but somehow there's
going to be another pile there again. Real soon.

Why do men leave piles? Perhaps, it goes back to survival
way back when there was the need to protect at a moment's
notice, so we felt the need to quickly get ready. Best way to
do that? Leave the important stuff in a pile near the sleeping
area.

So why fight with us about it?

You lose points and he's thinking, "If she doesn't like it,
why doesn't she pick them up?"

Yup, that's what he's thinking.

"What? Did Mr. Knuckle-dragger just say I should
become housekeeping like this is some sort of hotel and I'm
the maid!"

I'm not saying you have to leave a mint on the pillow.
What I am saying is to go the extra mile. Those who do it in
sports and business win. You can also win by doing it in a

133

relationship. Stop fighting windmills and start building a runway.

I dated a woman whose parents have been happily married for 36 years. Barbara and Hugh. Hugh is a doctor, and Barbara used to own her own business. Rarely will you ever see two people so in love. They still have many moments when they look at each other like it's the first time. If we could all have that, we would truly know what it's like to be in paradise. Their marriage works for many, many reasons. First and foremost, of course, is the chemistry they have with each other. The other reasons include their mutual respect for one another, manifesting in the things she does for him and the things he does for her.

Early on when they first got married, Barbara learned not to argue over things that weren't going to change and really weren't that big of a deal. Did I mention they've been happily married for 36 years? She would pick up his pile of clothes and put them in the hamper. You should know that Barbara is an independent woman who considers herself a feminist and was very active with the Women's Movement. She might kill me for telling you this stuff. Actually, she might kill her daughter for telling me this and telling me that Barbara loves to cook for her husband, has no problem giving her husband space and does many, MANY of the things I suggest in this book. Did I mention they've been happily married for 36 years?

Back to the 'clothes pile' story: After several years, Barbara had enough and decided to stop picking up Hugh's clothes. She didn't argue with him or say anything about it, she just figured he'd run out of clean underwear and finally pick them up and put them in the hamper. Nope. What did Hugh do? He bought new underwear! I'm laughing at this one because I have since found out lots of other men do this. My friend Amy said that her husband has like, 35 pairs of jeans. He wasn't even conscious that he was doing it. He just thought he ran out of jeans! He's a well-educated man, proving even intelligent men think like Neanderthal Men when it comes to certain things.

What did Barbara do? Did she pick a fight? No. She hired a housekeeper to pick up his piles of clothes. If they didn't have the money to hire a housekeeper, she would have gone back to picking them up. Did I mention they've been happily married for 36 years? She realized there was absolutely no sense in arguing over something so trivial.

Why not take a lesson from Barbara and Hugh, who, I'm not sure I mentioned this, have been happily married for 36 years. They worked together as a team. She did things for him, he did things for her, and together they built a rock-solid foundation that took mutual chemistry and turned it into Camelot.

Let's say you decided, "Oh, why not, I'll pick up the piles."

Why not try to have fun with it? Treat it like a game of Pick-Up Sticks. When we were kids that was a fun game. If we had to pick up a bunch of sticks now, we'd think it sucks. (This is true for many of the 'tasks' we do as adults and enjoyed doing as kids. Yes, that's another book.) Be a kid, have fun picking up his pile.

Okay, who am I kidding? If it were fun, we men would be picking them up! My advice is to either let the piles stay or take them away and not complain about it, so you don't 'Pile Drive' him to give you negative points.

At the end of the day, what's the big deal spending five minutes picking up some clothes, compared to a lifetime of happy memories?

By the way, did I mention that Barbara and Hugh have been happily married for 36 years?

POINT VALUE: Plus six subconscious points if you don't say anything. Minus three if you consistently get down on him for doing it.

FOR THE SIX MEN READING THIS BOOK: You're all a bunch of lazy knuckle-draggers who could pick up your piles from time to time and—who am I kidding? I'm not going to do it, why should I expect you to do it? Okay, how's this? We'll both do it on special occasions; like her birthday, anniversary or after she takes the time to do something for us, like, uh, put up with us, leaving piles of clothing on the floor.

He Scores!!! You Don't

When He's Watching Sports, He's Not
Interested in Anything Else.

*"Freedom is not worth having if it does not include the
freedom to make mistakes."*
— Gandhi
(Peacemaker. Trailblazer. World Changer)

AS I stated earlier, one of the things I want to do when I tell
you how we men think is protecting your heart from the many,
many, many, many, many, many, many and did I mention
MANY times that we men don't think. When it comes to
watching sports, not only don't we men think, we don't hear
or see very well either—unless it's the sport we're watching.
Playing them, we hear and see you great because we want you
there, cheering on our manhood!

Why are sports so important to most men? (As you know
this book is about how to get a man. I know how important
sports are for women, both playing and watching. In fact, I
wish all women played sports growing up because studies
show the MANY benefits and positive effects it has for
women). One reason it's important for men is that men still
have the need to be warriors and we can vicariously be
warriors by playing sports and watching other 'warriors' go
to 'war'. The main reason is that much of the bonding we did
with our dad and our friends while growing up was through
watching, talking, and/or playing sports. We men don't like
to show that deeper side of us, especially to other men,
especially to other men who aren't our best friend. Even if
they are, we don't like doing it. We bond by talking about
sports—or quoting lines from movies. Why is this important
to know? Because *"in order to get a gopher, you need to think*

like a gopher, act like a gopher and whenever possible, look like a gopher." (Bill Murray in 'Caddyshack'.) For your purposes, other than "looking like a gopher", just replace the word 'gopher' with 'man'.

A man can remember a line from a movie he saw seventeen centuries ago easier than your birthday, anniversary, or the names of co-workers. Why? That one is beyond reason.

Like Paul Newman said to Robert Redford in "Butch Cassidy and the Sundance Kid", "I got vision and the rest of the world wears bifocals."

In this area, I'm in bifocal land.

When it comes to watching sports, men become 'bifocaled'. All we see is the game. (We can eat during it— I'll get to that shortly, text, check stats and fantasy stats but that is still part of the sports-watching experience. Anything else is a distraction and we tune it out, get annoyed or both). If you're not a fan of the sport your man loves and you don't want to waste away the day watching with him, no need to get your feelings hurt or into an argument because you want to talk to him while he's conquering the world. Wait until the 'war' is over. You might be able to have a conversation during commercials, but you won't have his full attention and it will end as soon as the game begins. Protect your feelings, and your sanity, and wait until he's done watching the game.

If the man you want is a football fan, and you're not, here is some useful information. Football season is only 16 games long, then three weeks of playoffs and the Super Bowl. Not many games compared to most other sports, so football time to a football fan is precious, especially if he's watching his favorite team. That means it is 'downtime' for the two of you.

Sometimes, even when it comes to sex.

Here's a true story about a woman who got her feelings hurt by an insensitive, idiot asshole who wasn't thinking. I'd like to point out that I fully believe this freakin' idiot asshole has learned from his mistake and will never, ever, ever do this again. Ever! Let's call this idiot asshole, uh...me. I hate confessing this, but as I said, I better be able to reveal my skeletons if I'm revealing society's.

I was dating Farrah. (Although I am not using her real name, I asked her if I could tell this story and she said, 'Yes'.) One morning, I woke up and went into the living room to watch a Giants football game. I'm a huge Giants fan. During the second half of a close game, she came in and wanted to do more of what we did the previous night. I turned down the sound and we started making out for a bit. Not sure how long, my guess was about one-eighth of a second. Like I said, I'm not proud of this, but I was in 'Unenlightened Bifocal Idiot Land' and I wanted to get back to it. I can't remember when or even how we got naked and started going at it, but we did.

During the thrusting phase, she caught me taking a peek at the TV, "Are you watching the game?"

I tried to cover and say I wasn't, but she wasn't buying it. She was really asking me a rhetorical question. She was really angry! I mean REALLY angry! In reality, she was hurt because I was saying the game was more important than she was. It wasn't, but I was an idiot asshole and I hurt her.

Farrah and I are no longer going out, but I am happy to say we are very good friends.

Originally, I wasn't going to write this chapter because I thought maybe it was just me. But then I checked with my guy friends who are sports fans and it turned out my stupidity was not an anomaly. Many of them said that they had done bifocal-land-idiot-asshole stuff like that.

One told me about the time he brought his mini TV, to be used in an emergency like an earthquake—or apparently a football game, to an expensive restaurant to finish watching Sunday Night Football while he was having an intimate anniversary dinner with his girlfriend. Yes, she was pissed. (Again, she was really hurt, but it manifested as anger). Another guy told me a similar story to mine. His girlfriend wanted to have sex, but a baseball game was coming on. He was smart enough not to start something he wasn't ready to finish and told her he would jump her as soon as the game was over. Then he was dumb enough not to jump her as soon as the game was over and watched Sports Center.

Don't put yourself in situations where there is a chance you will get hurt.

It's not that sports are more important than you, or sex, or anything else that really matters. It's not even close. It's just men who enjoy sports sometimes don't see the bigger picture. In the case of football, the season is a total of five months. Sounds like a lot but out of those five months, most days and nights are free. Sunday is game day and night. There is also a game on Monday and Thursday night (which the NFL should get rid of). The rest of the week is free and clear. There are two games on Thanksgiving Day, two weekends of Saturday games during the playoffs. If your man is also into college football, those games are on Saturdays and I can't begin to explain or figure out what day or night the bowl games are played.

Okay, as I write this, it sounds like a LOT of freakin' football. It's not as bad as it sounds. If you add up all the hours, it's not that much time and most of it is on Sunday.

Some of you are thinking, "What about baseball season, Mr. Knuckle-dragger, or basketball? How about hockey?" Different. There are way more than 16 games. In baseball, there are 162 regular season games. Basketball, 82. Hockey, also 82.

If you're doing the math right now, you're going, "Mr. Knuckle-dragger, $16+162+82+82 = 342$. There are 365 days in a year. That leaves 23 days for us women!" Any guy watching that much sports should be watching from a padded room.

POINT VALUE: Plus three if you understand bifocal land. Minus five if you get into an argument over it.

FOR THE SIX MEN READING THIS BOOK: Dude, if your woman wants to make love during a game, really, how much time are you going to be away from the TV? 20 minutes? 25? Who am I kidding! It won't take that long. You'll skip the foreplay and get right to it. Who am I kidding, you always skip the foreplay and get right to it! So, what's the big deal about missing two maybe two and a half minutes of a game to be with your woman? For those who can't miss any of the game, get DVR so you never ever put her in that situation. You'll get to watch the game, skip past the annoying commercials, and make your woman happy. Triple/Double.

Nacho, Nacho Man

Men Like to Snack while Watching TV, So
Why Not Make Him Something?

*"Progress in civilization has been accompanied by progress
in cookery."*
— Fannie Farmer
(Her ground-breaking cookbook, 'The Boston Cooking-
School Cook Book' made life easier for domestic cooks,
who were, for the most part, women.)

NO one knows my whereabouts and I got rid of the Mulberry
Pizza delivery guy 'cause I found out he could be bribed, so
remember that before you come gunning for me. Make the
man you want something to eat so he can nosh during the
game. I ducked because I know at least one of you; check that,
probably many of you threw this book at my head.

Don't throw the book. Go the extra mile, in this case, not
a long mile at all, and take 30 seconds to throw a bunch of
nachos in a bowl, another 30 seconds to dump a jar of salsa in
another bowl and another 30 seconds to slide it on the coffee
table near him. A minute and a half to score easy points. If
you want, you can just toss the bag of nachos and the jar of
salsa in front of him and cut the whole process down to fifteen
seconds. As long as it's in his reach, he's going to eat it and
appreciate it.

The secret is, all these 'little' things I'm suggesting you
do to help you, become a habit. By becoming a habit, you are
planting your own seeds. Once planted, you can watch them
grow until a bouquet is formed—a bouquet that you can toss
to someone else, (along with this book) as you leave the
wedding chapel!

POINT VALUE: Plus two

FOR THE SIX MEN READING THIS BOOK: Hey, Nacho Head, if your woman tosses nachos or whatever into a bowl for you, you should be tossing her some roses when she's least expecting it—as well as hugs and kisses and compliments. Points will be scored, and you will be adored! (Damn, that was corny.)

My Dream Is to Marry Pigpen!

Don't Be a Slob

"The problem with people who have no vices is that generally, you can be pretty sure they're going to have some pretty annoying virtues."
— Elizabeth Taylor
(Academy Award-winning actor, AIDS activist)

I know I wrote that men will leave piles of clothing on the floor and that you should let it slide; however, most men won't cut you the same slack. We're the Pile Clothes Makers—you're not. We can be slobs—you should be clean and sparkly. Unfair? Yes. But it's the way it is. Do you want to fight windmills?

Why do we men expect women to be clean and clean up after us? Why do men have the nerve to think it's natural for women to be clean and men to be messy? Why does this stereotype exist? I believe it's because way back when, while us men were outside the cave smoking a leaf with our buddies to celebrate the birth of our newborn, you ladies not only gave birth to the baby, you cleaned up after the birth and you cleaned the baby. If you hadn't, infection would have formed, and the baby wouldn't have survived... neither would the human race.

From the beginning, *you cleaned up the mess we made.*

Besides your personal appearance, the place you live is your sanctuary. Treat it like one. If you have so much stuff it's overflowing, get rid of it. (Please don't throw it out. Give it to charity.) The half-eaten sandwich you can throw out. I 'purge' my place several times a year, especially at Christmas. I cannot begin to tell you the expressions of joy you'll get when you bring those items to a shelter. It will warm you to your very core. Triple/Double.

Your car is also an extension of you. Clean out the junk in your trunk.

Many people believe in Feng Shui, the art of placing things in certain areas to displace negative energy and increase positive energy. I believe that's possibly true. I know if you believe it to be so, it IS so. I do fully believe that when you make your environment more pleasing to all your senses, you are happier and healthier. So, you're not just doing this for him, you're doing it for you. Again, Triple/Double.

If the place you live is your sanctuary, your bed is the shrine. If you're going to invite us into your shrine, make sure there's not crap all over it or it's full of crumbs. Yes, we're men, and we're not going to kick you out of bed for eating crackers. But we'd prefer not to have saltines up our ass.

William, a guy I knew, had a massive crush on this woman. Turns out she liked him too. They went on a date arranged by mutual friends. After their date, William escorts her back to her car and it is a mess. She immediately gets negative points.

Date two: William picks her up and, being a gentleman, goes to her door to escort her to his car. He sees the inside of her apartment, which is very messy. That ends William's crush and the chance of a relationship to blossom.

Maybe the guy you want isn't as anal as William, but why chance it? Again, little things make big differences. You want every advantage you can get. I don't know any guy who says, "I met the perfect woman! She's a slob! I always wanted a freakin' slob! I always dreamed of marrying Pigpen!!!"

SUBCONSCIOUS POINT VALUE: Plus three. Minus five if you're a slob.

FOR THE SIX MEN READING THIS BOOK: Like any of you should talk. If "Godliness is next to cleanliness", you might as well pack now for down under.

Wax on, Wax Off

> Don't Let Your Man See You Fixing Yourself Up

"The secrets a woman has to make herself more beautiful are just that."

— Unknown

YOU ladies already know this, but it's worth stating. We men don't need to know your trade secrets. We men have no idea how much time and effort you spend enhancing your looks. Nor should we.

Do you really want us to know that you wax this on and wax this off? Do you want us to know you whiten, pluck, spray tan, Botox, weave, nip, tuck, staple, or many other things you might do? Sure, we know it. Fine, great, not a problem. We just don't want to see it.

Put away all that, uh, 'stuff' lying all over your bathroom counter. Don't answer the door with white paste over your upper lip. Hairnets are to be worn in the cafeteria. I, for one, never understood how, at one time, it became a fashion statement. But maybe that's just me. I think a woman looks sexy in a Santa hat, so what do I know?

Grant your man that illusion, because, in reality, it's not an illusion at all. That beauty is already there. All that stuff simply enhances it, many times because of how you feel inside. Confidence is powerful.

Sure, when the Wonder Bra eventually comes off, he's going to wonder where 'they' went. But by then, it's no big deal. ☺

POINT VALUE: Minus six if you insist on letting the man you want in on your trade secrets.

144

FOR THE SIX MEN READING THIS BOOK: Hey, monkey boy, it might not hurt for you to get rid of that hair you're sprouting in unnecessary places or to trim that Brillo Pad Jungle around Mini Me. She'll have a better shot of finding him and he'll look less mini. Triple/Double! Get a manicure every now and then; and for The Universe's sake, cut those claws on your toes so when the evening turns to night, she doesn't think she's in bed with a Werewolf!

Now I am not saying to become a 'Metrosexual Man'. That crap was created by advertisers to get men to buy more and more stuff until we're wearing lip gloss and mascara and it's not because we're about to become the next Prince or Ozzy. Not that there is anything wrong if you want to wear lip-gloss and/or mascara. I feel wearing a Kilt is very, uh, freeing. I could be all wet about this one, but I don't think you ladies want to hear, "I'll be over as soon as I'm done removing my eye cream and buffing out my balls." (Okay, maybe you'd like the buffing out thing.) I think (I don't know for sure 'cause I'm not a woman), but I think women like a guy who's not afraid to be a little rough around the edges. Case in point, here's a tip for you fellow grunters. A study in Esquire Magazine (March 2006) showed that almost 70% of women think the "sexiest thing a man can wear" is not a suit or tuxedo; it's "rugged jeans and a t-shirt." Let's be honest ladies, who would you rather be with, David Beckham or Tucker Carlson? (Okay, bad example because, does anyone want to be with Tucker Carlson?)

That being said, guys, it wouldn't be a bad idea that when you finally get a shot to go to The Promised Land, you don't strip down forgetting that you happen to put on your Harry Potter boxer briefs that day. (Yes, that happened to someone I know. That someone being me. A woman I dated gave them to me and... okay, I'm not going to make any excuses. I like them!) Also, make sure you're wearing underwear that doesn't have holes, and your tighty-whitey's are just that; tidy and white.

Your Sixth Sense

We All Have Six Senses: Sight, Sound, Touch, Taste, Smell, and Our Sixth Sense. You Can Use All Six to Get a Man Because Consciously or Not, He Will Take Note on How You Present Yourself in All These Areas

"Life begets life. Energy creates energy. It is by spending oneself that one becomes rich."

– Sarah Bernhardt
(Legendary stage and screen actor)

WE were given our six senses not only to enhance our enjoyment of life but mainly to help us survive. We don't use them enough. We especially don't use as many as we can at once, which is a shame because when we do, we feel totally alive.

Great athletes know this. In order to be at the top of their game, they must use sight, sound, touch—even taste and smell— (they can taste victory and smell fear). That sixth sense comes in mighty handy when you feel in your gut that he's going to throw a fastball, because if you're right and he does, you just hit a home run.

Great cooks understand that an amazing meal is not just about taste. It's also about sight, smell, touch, sound... and your sixth sense (gut). An example of this is Chinese Sizzling Rice Soup. I love that sizzling sound. The sight of the rice melting into the hot broth is really cool. The smell is great. The touch on my tongue feels warm. The taste is amazing. I feel happy and content when I'm done eating it. Why not be a great cook and cook YOURSELF into a great meal that pleases all six senses of the man you want?

SIGHT: When a man sees a woman he is attracted to, her image goes at 1,000,000,000,000,000,000x's light speed from his eyes, past his heart (at times skipping a beat), and ends up in his dick. If our dicks could see, we'd save a step.

Take time to look your best when you're out on the prowl. Hey, why not do this when you're not on the prowl? You never know when that window of opportunity will open and Mr. Dreamboat will crawl through it. Whatever your body type, height, age, etc., look your personal best because you will feel good about yourself and in the process look much better.

Why? 'Confidence'.

No matter what you wear, confidence gets you everywhere. I'm not saying you can't be a coy if you want. Just make sure there's confidence in your coyness.

My friend Sydney is a full-figured woman. She was telling me how she hates LA because no guys ever look at her. I told her it was because she lacked confidence. She told me it was because she was fat. After much effort, I convinced her to wear something that was sexier than she usually does with confidence. Not something sleazy, but something that makes her feel good about herself—not the cover-up stuff she normally wears. She finally did it and was CONFIDANT. Lo and behold, she got more attention from guys then she had in a very long time.

Confidence is a very powerful tool.

I'm not saying you have to be dressed to the nines every time you leave your house. You could be in jeans or shorts, messy hair or styled hair. Different things work for different people. Just make sure whatever you wear flatters you. For those ladies who have the No Fashion Sense, What-So-Ever gene like me, ask an ally to aid you, so you don't have people wondering why the Fashion Police haven't arrested you yet.

Remember: men look with their cock first. And second. And third. And...

POINT VALUE: Infinite. This is the starting gate.

SOUND: If you saw 'When Harry Met Sally', you laughed at the scene when Meg Ryan faked an orgasm because you know you've done it and you know your man thinks he's the only one you've ever done it with. I love that

147

moan of ecstasy during the heat of passion. I hope it is real. I know it isn't always. But like any man, even though I just said, "I know it isn't," I really believe it is real. Most men love some kind of sound from women. Some men like moaning or cooing, screaming or finding out that God has suddenly become a big part of your life. Makes us feel like men!

Then there's talking dirty. If you've waited to give away the milk, you might have a very good idea if and what your man likes when it comes to this subject.

Other little sounds you surround yourself with can be a big plus. Like music, as long as it's music you both like. Otherwise, it sucks and is annoying to listen to. A water fountain can be soothing as well. You can get inexpensive tabletop ones. Or you can get an app with sounds of fountains, birds chirping, wind howling, fireplace crackling, the ocean, etc. Why bother? Again, your sanctuary should be as pleasing as possible. If he likes the sounds of you and your house… guess where he's going to want to spend his time?

Another great sound is the sound of silence. When I first started doing stand-up, a comedian said to me, "You'll know you're a pro when you're comfortable with the silence." I had no idea what he was talking about because the last thing I wanted was silence. Then, one day on stage, I did a bit and people weren't laughing. I realized they were listening—that I had their undivided attention. When I hit them with the 'punch', the silence, in this case, was deafening. The comedian was right. I LOVED it. Because I said something so true they wanted to absorb it. Then I went on to get laughs. The same goes for a relationship. When you're with your man and neither of you feel the need and feel you don't have to say anything—you're both cool with just being—you've become comfortable with the silence. Then you've gone to the next level. A level that can take your relationship to the peak of the highest mountain.

SUBCONSCIOUS POINT VALUE: Plus four

<u>TOUCH</u>: No better feeling for a man than the feeling of the woman we love in our arms. Or to touch her lips, her face, her arms, legs, etc. Smooth and soft = nice. Like I said, I'm not pulling punches or caving to PC pressure. Make all the statements you want by not shaving, but with all due respect

to French women, if you want to land a man most American men are looking to groove with someone smooth.

SUBCONSCIOUS POINT VALUE: Plus eight

TASTE: Besides your cooking, we like to taste you. Many of us, everywhere. Your lips, neck, ears, breasts, thighs, stomach and beyond. Or is that below? Anyway, make sure you taste good. Everywhere.

POINT VALUE: Plus ten

SMELL: Many smells make us feel happy and safe. As Helen Keller said, *"Smell is a potent wizard that transports you across thousands of miles and all the years you have lived."*

A smell that does this for me is pipe tobacco. My grandfather smoked a pipe and that smell brings with it memories of a fun day of fishing and eating bologna and ketchup sandwiches. It brings a smile to my face.

Why not make you a familiar, happy, safe feeling, great-smelling, habit-forming, big-smile-to-his-face scent?

Remember, your place and your car are an extension of you. Make sure they smell good. You can choose from many scents. For example, a scent men love is the smell of a home-cooked meal. (Am I in trouble, again?)

Another scent I remember is Lily. Lily smelled great—everywhere. Lily not only scored big subconscious points on the plus side, but she also got to spend a lot more time on her back enjoying me, uh, pleasuring her. Unfortunately, she lost way too many points in other areas for the relationship to last.

This leads to a HUGELY, MASSIVELY, INCREDIBLY IMPORTANT area we need to talk about. Bad scents also bring back memories, as well as keep us away from more possible moments and memories.

Thus, I need to talk about a particular scent. Your vagina. It MUST not smell bad!

There, I said it.

Well, actually, I wrote it—but that didn't make it much easier to 'say'—Why? Guys are VERY UNCOMFORTABLE talking about this subject TO A WOMAN. We have ABSOLUTELY NO PROBLEM WHAT-SO-EVER GRUNTING ABOUT IT AMONGST OURSELVES.

Understand, a bad smelling uh, vajaja is not common. It is the exception to the rule. But why risk being that exception? This is one rule you do not want to be an exception to. Little things make a huge difference, and this is not a little thing and it can make all the difference. Even if a man really likes you, he'd rather move to another planet than say, "Honey, your vajaja doesn't smell so good."

How do you know if you smell bad? I really have no idea. I guess if he goes down on you once but never to return… you can ask him. I'm pretty sure he's not going to tell you the truth. Actually, forget about asking him. He's not going to tell you the truth unless the truth is, "Honey, you smell great!"

So actually, do ask him. If he stutters, stammers answers half-heartedly or changes the subject altogether, you have your answer.

There was a girl I was CRAZY about when I was 17. She was beautiful, sexy, and smart. I finally got up enough nerve to ask her out and she said, 'Yes'. I ran home, like five miles, I was so excited. We dated. One night, I was given a pass to The Promised Land. That night, the fantasy ended. Ten years later, I was talking with a good friend of mine. For some reason, her name came up, and I asked him if he'd ever been with her. He said, "Yes, and man did she smell bad!"

That's how long something like this can stick with you. That's how important it is to take care of your vajaja. Do what you can to make sure your scent is like a rose to his nose and not thorns because if we get to The Promised Land and it's not all that it's promised to be, we'll go hunting elsewhere.

POINT VALUE: Minus 10,000,0000,000 if you are the exception to the rule and you smell bad down there.

YOUR SIXTH SENSE: Also known as your 'gut' or your 'third eye'. This is your most important sense. Unfortunately, it's the least listened-to or used. I think this is because many people pooh-pooh it. They don't believe it actually exists. Why? Probably, because in modern society, especially in Western civilization, it's weird to use something that isn't tangible. To many, it seems mystical, and therefore magical and therefore hocus-pocus trickery.

Some think it goes against Judeo-Christian beliefs. In reality, it actually goes with those beliefs. Prayer is your sixth sense at work WHEN USED CORRECTLY. Meaning, you can't just go "Please God, I want this or that" You need to visualize it, feel it, and not give up on that feeling. I don't believe in organized religion of any kind, but I do believe in "Magic". That magic is a connection we all have with the energy that is our Universe. You can use that energy to better your life. Again, another book for another day) Gaining insights from some higher power is your sixth sense tuned in; which is why your sixth sense is NEVER wrong.

POINT VALUE: Infinite for you, personally. This is because it can be used in all areas to keep you out of trouble and better your life. When you listen to it, you not only score major points with him but more importantly—yourself.

FOR THE SIX MEN READING THIS BOOK: As far as smell and taste go, a female friend of mine who read a draft said (and I am paraphrasing), if the junk stinks the junk doesn't get anywhere near her mouth or nose. If what comes out Mr. Longbow tastes nasty, blowjobs are a thing of the past.

As far as all your six senses go: Don't just see with your eyes, see with your heart. Don't hear what you want to say, listen to what she needs to say. Remember that your touch is something she craves. If you're with a woman who puts what I wrote in this book to use, wake up, smell the roses and give your six senses a place to call home. Her.

Use the Force

Trust Your Sixth Sense. It Is Never Ever Wrong.

"A person who thinks they can and a person who thinks they can't, are both right."

– Unknown

LUKE Skywalker in Star Wars had all this amazing technology he could use to help him defeat the Death Star. In the end, he used nothing but his Sixth Sense, known in the movie as, 'The Force'. The Force was the infinite wisdom of The Universe, transferred to him. I know, I sound like a major geek using 'Star Wars' as a reference. But Sir George Lucas understood a lot about what The Universe has to offer to all those who believe and are willing to use Her.

There's no book, computer, website, piece of information, piece of technology, teacher, or anything else we have or can create that compares to the power of our sixth sense. It is never wrong. When you're in tune with it, you know the answer so well, it burns inside of you. Whether it comes to a man being full of crap, or an idea you have that will make you millions—you know it to be true and you feel it in every part of your body.

Unfortunately, most times, we don't listen to it. LISTEN TO IT! *LISTEN TO YOUR SIXTH SENSE.*

Did your gut ever tell you: "Don't park in this spot," but you did it anyway, only to come back and find a dent or a ticket? I have. Or how about the time you felt you shouldn't buy something, but you did anyway, only to regret it later? Yep, done that, been there. Oh well, uh, I know! How about the many times your gut told you, "Don't go out with him!",

"Dump him!", "Run!" but you didn't listen because you stared into his dreamy eyes, heard the words you wanted to hear, saw the things you wanted to see, allowed your other senses to overwhelm and push back your most important one.

I once dated a woman who lived with her mom and cats and I can't explain what it was, but the energy was weird, and my gut told me to run—but I didn't. On our third date, she and her mom (and possibly one of the cats) cornered me to tell me I was chosen by God to produce their TV show. As I listened, I thought if there is a God, he had a lot better things to do than choose me to get this really lame idea of theirs on TV.

By being more in tune with your Sixth Sense, you are opening the greatest instrument ever created, 'the human body', to pull in the greatest force there is, 'the collective consciousness of The Universe" So use it as often as you can.

Many times, it is hard to differentiate between your Sixth Sense and all that stuff inside your head and those feelings inside your heart. They get in the way and you get emotional and reactionary. When you're not sure, when you keep going back and forth on a decision, that's your Sixth Sense working on overdrive to try and override your head and heart. When this happens, shut all else out, close your eyes, let your mind go and ask your higher power to supply you with the answer. This means you have to put down the TV remote, computer, cell, iPad and Starbucks cappuccino frappé latte, whatever-'atte', and focus on not focusing on anything—other than the faith that you will be given the answer for which you ask. Most of us know that old saying, "Ask and ye shall receive." Yet, so few of us ever do it.

I grew up in New Jersey and New York, not California or Mars (same place to many people), so I was once a skeptic. Perhaps, you are to. However, I have come to realize through events in my life that there are forces, good ones that work for us when we want them to.

For our purposes, when the man you're with says things to you that you aren't quite sure are real, listen with your sixth sense or that other name it goes by: Your 'Bullshit Detector'. Sure, it's great to hear a guy say nice things and if that's your only agenda, enjoy it. If you have a broader agenda like, let's say, to land a man, you need to make sure his agenda isn't to just lay pipe.

Now if you'll excuse me, I'm a little tired. I'm going to go put on my Star Wars PJ's, brush my teeth with my Game of Thrones toothbrush, jump into my Spider-Man bed, pull up my Speed Racer sheets, fluff out my Bugs Bunny pillows, set my Snoopy alarm clock and click off my New York Giants lamp.

Hey, maybe I am more of a major geek than I realized!

POINT VALUE: Infinite if you listen to your sixth sense. Finite if you don't. FOR THE SIX MEN READING THIS BOOK: Ditto.

Life is Stranger than Fiction

There is No Such Thing as Impossible.
Anything is Possible as Long as You Believe it
Is

"Build it and he will come."
– Field of Dreams
(Book by W. P. Kinsella, Screenplay by Phil Robinson)

OKAY, maybe I don't really have a Spider-Man bed or Bugs Bunny pillows—anymore. But I am drinking tea from my Skywalker Ranch Mug! (I really am.) Last night, my gut told me I was forgetting some Yodaesque subject I want to talk to you about. I asked The Universe for the answer right before I went to sleep. I thought about the question and had the faith I would get the answer. Sleep is a powerful tool not used to its fullest potential. It is the link between this world and others. It is the light where there is a void. It can link us to people no longer here. It can provide the answers that we seek.

So, before I went to sleep, I planted a seed by asking The Universe, "What am I forgetting to say?" That seed turned into a dream. And within that dream was my answer. (NOTE: This doesn't always work. But it works a lot and a lot more if you work it).

Last night, I had a dream that I was hanging with Kevin Costner. When I woke up, it didn't take me too long to figure out what that dream meant. 'Field of Dreams', a movie Costner starred in, is about a man who follows his gut, even when others think he has gone crazy. More importantly, not only did he follow it, he followed through. He did what he had to do in order to get what he so desperately needed.

I don't believe in the word 'impossible'. In fact, I HATE that word. I wish it was banned, especially when we're young and we still dare to dream the 'impossible'. I believe that you can accomplish anything you set out to accomplish, you just have to SEE what it is you want, FEEL what it would be like to have it, FOCUS on getting it and BELIEVE you can attain it. Then, it's already yours and all you have to do is claim it.

How does 'just' thinking about something build anything? Thought is energy. Energy is looking to become matter. Your focused thoughts can turn energy into matter and dreams into reality.

Too many dreams die early deaths. One of those is when women start to think they will never be with the right man, or never get married—or never marry a man they truly want. Have no fear, hope is here! Right here—in this book.

Ask, (believe) and know you shall receive. Which is also another way of saying "energy turns into matter." Science, like religion, requires faith to find the truth. Unlike religion, science requires facts to establish the truth. Two facts are: energy can never die, and faith is a powerful thing. Without it, we'd accomplish nothing.

Let's pause here. I'd like you to put down this book or turn off the audio if you are listening to it and write out what kind of man you want to meet and what kind of life you want to have with him. Don't hold back. Let your dreams and imagination flow. You should feel happy and excited as you write. If you're not, stop, see what you really want, believe it, and start writing again. You're creating the man of your dreams. You'd better be excited!

You can't just think about it. It must hit you emotionally. You must feel it. Once you've written out your dream man, I'd like you to read it out loud, twice a day; once before bed and once right after you wake up. Your brain is sleepy, so you can bypass many of its fears and have the faith that he's out there and he's already yours. All you need do is claim him.

Another reason I love sports and why I use sports as an analogy so much is because you must have the faith that you can win, in order to win. If you don't you've lost before the match has even begun. We all feel like underdogs, thus, the reason we root for them. We INSTINCTIVELY understand that, although we might be underdogs, many times faith overcomes odds. On those special occasions, we get to watch David slay Goliath.

In the 1980 Olympics, the U.S.A. Hockey Team was out-matched in every area by the Russian Hockey Team. The Russians were professionals and we were kids. They were feared and we were jokes. They had a seasoned team that had not lost to any opponent in recent history. We had a ragtag group, who was put together by a coach, many thought was crazy. Yet, in those Olympics, the 'impossible' happened and our hockey team took home the gold.

"Do you believe in miracles?" shouted Al Michaels. Yes, yes, I do.

In Super Bowl 42, the 12-6 New York Giants beat the 18-0 New England Patriots. (As I mentioned I'm a huge Blue fan, so I had to get this in here.) This was one of the all-time biggest upsets in Super Bowl and sports history.

Many of our greatest athletes became so even though most "experts" said they never would. They did so by overcoming obstacles or a lack of skills because they believed (and worked hard to turn obstacles into pathways). Athletes like; Danica Patrick (race car driver), Mike Piazza (baseball player), Margo Oberg (surfer), Jackie Robertson (baseball player), Russell Wilson (quarterback), Billie Jean King (tennis), to name just a very few.

They all achieved what they did because they didn't listen to naysayers and they were HONEST WITH THEMSELVES. If they had a weakness, they'd admit it to themselves, then turn lemons into lemonade by working on any 'weaknesses' they had and exploiting them to their advantage.

One more example. This person isn't a famous athlete, but he did overcome perceived obstacles to win. My guess is pretty much everyone said to him; "Are you freakin' crazy? Have you looked at the color of your skin? Have you looked at your name? It will never happen!"

This person would NOT listen to 'conventional wisdom'. By not listening, he proved all the naysayers wrong. So next time you feel like a victim and/or people say to you, "Can't," or "Won't ever happen" or "Impossible"—I'd like you to think of these three words: "Barack Hussein Obama." A man of color, with a weird first name, a Muslim middle name and a weird last name, who went on to become the 44th President of the United States of America. A day, I'd like to add, I was *VERY* proud to be an American. (Another example of anything is possible is, sadly, America's 45th president. If someone like that can become president—wow, anything truly is possible! Needless to say, when he won, this was not a day I was proud to be an American, a man... or part of the human race. I know, I know. Another book for another time).

Nothing is 'impossible' as long as you don't give up. It took Edison 101 attempts to create the light bulb. At one time, you couldn't walk or read. Imagine your life if you had given up on that! Same goes with finding a man. It doesn't matter how many times you've tried or how many other self-help books you've read that didn't work for you. Perhaps, you didn't work them? Whatever the reasons, that's the past! Now and the future is all that matters. Learn from the past. Live in the moment. See the future you want... and have faith. Or as Tony Robins says, *"The past does not equal the future."*

If you think you are down and out, if you feel like Rocky before he was offered the fight against Apollo Creed, if you feel like Sally before she met Harry, or even if you are Sleepless in Seattle, I want you to KNOW that you can accomplish the 'impossible', no matter how many times you tried and 'failed'. In actuality, you never fail until you give up on something you want.

What does any of this have to do with getting a man? I want you to be fully aware and totally understand that *YOU ALREADY HAVE THE POWER TO CHANGE YOUR LIFE*. All you need to do is use it.

Okay, that will conclude the Yoda-jD portion of the book. Yes, I can go into more detail like, what you think is who you are and what you attract... but I'm going to hand the Yoda reigns to three other people I have learned a lot from through their work. I strongly suggest you read or get programs from Tony Robins, read Napoleon Hill's, "Think and Grow Rich" and read "The Power of Your Subconscious Mind" by Dr. Joseph Murphy. All incredibly excellent teachers who I continue to learn from because, like this book, it's good to read them or listen to them more than once. They are invaluable.

POINT VALUE: Infinite if you believe and act upon those beliefs. Finite if you don't.

FOR THE SIX MEN READING THIS BOOK: Ditto.

Okey-Dokey

Don't Tell Him You Want to Get Married

"I don't need a man to justify my existence. The most profound relationship we'll ever have is the one with ourselves."
— Shirley MacLaine
(Academy Award-winning actor, author, and possible extra-terrestrial)

IF you're 25 or older, men automatically assume you want to get married. If you're over 30, men think you not only want to get married but that you spend every spare moment trying to. Whether men are right or wrong is not the issue. What matters is for you to know what men think. Why tell your man what he thinks he already knows when the relationship is new and you're still getting to know one another?

If you don't say it, he's going to start to wonder why you haven't said it, because he's so used to it being said to him by like, an hour into the first date, "I'd like to get married one day."

If you don't say it for at least the first six months, he's going to feel a little insecure and vulnerable. Not a bad thing for him to feel because he's going to start to wonder, which means *you have him thinking about the subject of marriage.*

Wait for your man to ask, "Do you ever want to get married?" Then, shock the hell out of him and say, "Only if the right man comes along. If I don't find that special man, I'm fine on my own."

After your man comes to, he will press you, thinking you're playing possum—that you're bluffing. He'll grunt, 'Really?' Don't give away your hand. Smile, shrug, move onto a new subject. Now, you're speaking his language. He'll believe you.

In poker, you never show your hand, because you would never win and lose what money you have in front of you. Don't show your hand. Don't have any 'tells'. [6]

This is not playing games. This is you understanding that there is no need to scare him off before he has a chance to really see how wonderful you are.

If your relationship continues to move forward, your man won't feel like he's just some sperm donor and cuddle toy that happened to be with you—or near you when you were ready. He'll feel like he's the one and only special man that came along!

POINT VALUE: Plus seven and a half if you say nothing. Minus six if you tell him too quickly.

FOR THE SIX MEN READING THIS BOOK: She read this book. She knows what you like. She deals with your crap. Marry her, you freakin' moron.

---

[6]Tells are little things poker players do subconsciously that give things away to their opponents; rub the brim of their hat, play with their glasses, crack their knuckles, bite their upper lip, cough, blink, etc.

Shit or Get off the Pot

Never Ever, Ever Tell Him He Must Marry
You or Else

*"I pay very little regard... to what any young person says on
the subject of marriage. If they profess a disinclination for
it, I only set it down that they have not yet seen the right
person."*

– Jane Austen

I am most certainly not saying that you should never talk to
your man about marriage. After you've spent some time
together, like at least six months, and you think this is the man
you want to marry, but you're still not sure what his intentions
are, you have every right to ask. Of course, if you don't know
what his intentions are after six months, you haven't been
very 007.

Don't ever threaten, cry, give him an ultimatum or back
him into a corner. (Remember the Roadrunner?) No guy
wants to feel that kind of pressure because then he feels caged
and trapped and all those terms you don't want popping back
into his head. You spent too much time getting them out of
his head and getting you into his heart. Why blow it by getting
anxious and yanking that fishing line too soon?

The best way for marriage to enter a man's mind is to let
his feelings sneak up on him. Try to hold out and let him be
the first to talk about it, let it happen organically.

If you must ask, be smart about it. Don't come out of the
gate saying, "Do you ever see yourself married to me?" Say,
"I see a future with you." Leave it at that. LISTEN to how he
acts and WATCH how he reacts for the next several months.
If he is distant and not as attentive, that's a good indication
that he's not interested in marrying you. At least not yet.

No one likes feeling rushed. Not him, not you, no one. Think about it. What if, while he was waiting for you to, let's say, have sex with him and he grunted, "Honey, you have one more month to give me a slice of heaven or I'm out of here for good!" You'd feel pressure. You might give up the goods. It might even be wonderful. But there is a chance that part of you will always resent that he pressured you into having sex and couldn't wait until you were ready. It will come up in an argument. It will surface.

By pressuring a man to get married, you might win the game but there is a very good chance you will lose the championship. Remember, you want a healthy, loving, life-lasting relationship.

You want a man to be in a marriage he *wants* to be in, not one he feels he has to be in. Needless to say, if a man pressures you—same results. Yes, there are always exceptions. But, as exceptional as you are, do you really want to gamble with your heart to see if you are that exception?

Sure, a little nudging here and there is fine. But, no nagging. If you really feel the need to put on the 'full-court press',[7] then perhaps you should take a good long look at the relationship you're in to see if you're both on the same path.

Now, what if you've both talked about marriage, but suddenly, that talk is no longer spoken. He's being a little cagey and not bringing up the subject. Or he's reacting a little squirrelly when you do, even though he and you have already talked about it. What do you do then? Pressure him? Dump him? What?

My friend, Rachel, came to me for advice on this problem. After a year of dating, her boyfriend Cold Feet said he wanted to get engaged to her in around six months. So, they moved in together. Six months go by and Mr. Feet has not said anything about the engagement. Rachel is now feeling insecure because she thinks he no longer wants to marry her. She has every right to feel that way.

---

[7] In basketball, when the defense starts putting pressure on the offense as soon as they toss in the ball, instead of waiting until they get past mid-court, it's called a 'full-court press'.

She tells me she wants to say to Cold Feet, "Either we get married, or it's over."

But, she still loves him very much and, although they aren't married, the relationship is very good, and she would feel terrible if it ended.

There are times in life that it's worth taking a step backward to take great leaps forward. Especially in a relationship that's going well, but you're not getting what you totally want.

Every sport has some sort of 'last resort plays'. Football has 'The Hail Mary'. The quarterback will send everyone who is eligible to catch a pass into the end zone, then throw the ball as far as he can, hoping one of his guys will make a miraculous catch. This is done either at the end of a half or by the team that is losing at the end of a game. In hockey and soccer, it's when you pull the Goalie[8].

That's what the miracle, 1980 U.S. Olympic Hockey team did in game one. If they hadn't, game two wouldn't have meant very much and there would never have been a miracle.

Yes, most of the time these tactics don't work. But every once in a while, someone takes a calculated risk and hockey teams made up of boys beat men who are established champions. As mentioned, we all, women and men, feel like underdogs in some way, so we love it when David beats Goliath. We all love those fairy tale endings. Wait! Did I just say everyone, including *men love fairy tale endings*? Yes, it's true! Men do believe in 'Happily Ever After'. Well, in sports we do. But, if we do in sports, we can in 'real' life. Just something to put in the back of your mind and use to your advantage.

In a relationship, sometimes it's worth taking, what most would call 'a step backward' and doing a last resort play.

A lot of people won't agree with me on this one. But a lot of people are alone.

---

[8]You pull your Goalie if the game is almost over and your team is down. At that point, it's much more important that you have another offensive skater on the ice to score a goal than to have a defensive player protecting it.

To wit, I suggested to Rachel that she NOT give Cold Feet the ultimatum. He might say, "Okay, let's get married," but there will come a time when he will wonder if he made a mistake and then resents her for pressuring him: Like every time they have a problem, even a little one. I suggested she say to him something like; "I moved in with you because we talked about getting married. If you need more time to think about it, that's okay. But, I'm going to get my own place, so you can have the space you need to decide what you want. I'm not going to date anyone else, nor should you, until you've figured it out."

I then told her, to give herself a date as to how long she will give him, *but not to tell him that date.* That way, Mr. Feet is not feeling pressure from a ticking clock. So, if he decides he wants to get married, he's doing it for the right reasons.

Rachel really, REALLY wanted to tell him he had three months. I pleaded with her and finally convinced her not to.

She did everything I suggested except move out. She said moving out was too drastic and too expensive. She moved onto the couch in another room, telling him that she didn't want sex to confuse the issue. She also spent nights at girlfriend's places. He certainly wasn't thrilled, but he was cool with it. Why? She was giving him his space and giving him time to let him make an important decision *without putting any pressure on him.*

About three months later, I got a call from Rachel saying Cold Feet planned a last-minute trip with her to Vegas! (When they first talked about marriage, it turns out they both wanted a Vegas wedding.)

She had one concern, "What if he's only marrying me so he can have sex with me again?"

My response: "If you had a magic vajaja, he would have dropped to his knees and begged you to marry him the very moment Mini Him touched its magic. If, however, the incredibly unlikely reason he wants to marry you is just so he can have sex with you again, you have a magical vajaja and you never have to worry about losing him or being alone again. Ever." She was cracking up, but she got the point.

A couple of days later, I got an excited call from Rachel, announcing that she was married. She took a step backward, she gave him space and room to think, she put no pressure on him and she won big time.

If a man doesn't see what you have to offer him and how great you two would be together—is he really the person you want at your side and on your team? Yes, the talent pool for women isn't as large as it is for men, but there are other guys in the ocean. You will find a better one, because that one will *want to be with you* and not feel like he *has to be with* you— or else.

There are no guarantees any marriage will work. But at least you're not starting off on a bad foundation, built by pressure... because pressure will eventually find a way to escape.

While we're here, I'd like to take a moment to think about the phrase, "Shit or get off the pot!"

Not only is it an image I can personally do without; but eventually—everyone Shits AND gets off the pot.

POINT VALUE: Minus ten if you pressure him. (And eventually, a lot more negative points because it will come up again and again and...)

FOR THE SIX MEN READING THIS BOOK: If your woman puts pressure on you, tell her why you're not ready. Scared of commitment is not a reason—it's an excuse. There's something else going on and you have to be honest with her and maybe more importantly, yourself. If you're not ever going to marry her, be a stand-up guy and tell her. Let her get on with her life.

What Time Is It?

Timing Can Be Important. Understand When It is
and When You Can Use It to Your Advantage

*"Chance is always powerful. Let your hook be always cast;
in the pool where you least expect it, there will be a fish."*
– Ovid
(Latin writer. 43 BC–17 AD)

TIMING. Is it everything? No. Is it something? Yes. There are times when timing can be bad. A man meets a woman he loves and can actually see spending his life with, but he just isn't ready. New job. Building his career. Wants to stay focused. Fear. Of course, if you score enough points, that bad timing becomes good because he realizes that he has a partner who will help him stay focused while building his career and he has nothing to fear—except losing you.

More on that coming up. Right now, I want to talk about when good timing is handed to you like a gift-wrapped present.

One of those instances is when all his buddies start to get married. In a circle of friends, you will see when one gets married, their buddies, in many cases, quickly follow suit. This is what I call, "The Wedding Effect".

No, he's not just marrying you because his buddies are getting married. He's seeing that one of his friends 'took the plunge' and it's not so bad. His friend looks happy. His friend is starting a new chapter and, maybe, it's time he does too.

His brain is working overtime now, He goes from thinking, "I've got the life because I can go out with a different woman every night," to "I've got a great life because I have a special Jeannie to go home to who really loves me."

The grass is always greener. When his buddies are getting married, that green pasture is blooming with opportunity.

POINT VALUE: No real point value, as there is absolutely nothing you can do to force timing. That being said, you score big points for yourself if when his buddy gets married, you VERY SUBTLY show him how happy his buddy is.

FOR THE SIX MEN READING THIS BOOK: Look at how happy your buddies are. Okay, most of them, not the one who got pressured into it and is putting on a fake act. The ones who really wanted to make the leap and are happier than they've ever been. They found that special person they want to share their life with. Don't you want the same for yourself?

Baby Talk

> If You Want Children, Put the Thought of Having
> a Child in His Mind Without Saying a Word

*"If evolution really works, how come mothers only have two
hands?"*
— Milton Berle
(Comedian, television pioneer)

THE techniques in this book will not only work to help you
get a man but also maintain the man you already have. (Or is
that MANtain?) This chapter is geared toward women who
want to have children with a man. I mean with a man at your
side to raise a child. As far as I know, the only way to have a
child is with a man even if a man is not present at the time of
conception. So, you're either married or with a man *you know
wants to spend his life with you.*

I say, "You know wants to spend his life with you"
because you don't want a man to be with you or marry you
just because he wants kids. (Unless that's all you want from
him and he's aware of it.) Yes, many times having kids is part
of the equation as to why people get married. But you want it
to be part of a sum, not the total. Otherwise, you're just an
incubator and eventually, you won't be a happy one.

A woman's clock starts ticking at a very early age[9]. When
you hit puberty, nature whispers, "Find a man to procreate."
(Thus, the reason we need to educate kids on why being a kid
and having a baby is not a very good idea, and why the issue

---

[9] Before you throw the book at my head, I recognize that this won't
apply to all women as recent statistics indicate there is increasing
number who are choosing not to have children.

of teaching abstinence without teaching how to protect yourself from getting pregnant or worse, a fatal disease, is absolutely and utterly absurd.) Like I've said, we have instinctual wants, needs, and habits that go wayyyyyy back. They can't be beaten out of us just because someone says so. Mother Nature says differently and her say is louder and truer.

When you hit your 20s, nature calls, "Find a man to procreate!" You hit your 30s and nature is screaming at you to "FIND A MAN TO PROCREATE!!!!!!"

This is when many women start reacting instead of acting and planning. In many cases, logic gets tossed aside and you ladies panic and make bad choices.

Why does this happen? If you have a baby, *you will survive*… long after you are gone.

Ladies, try to remember, it's a ticking clock, not a ticking bomb. You don't need to panic. As you get older, there are gifts you possess that someone younger doesn't have. Wear these gifts proudly and you'll find a man who can't wait to open up his present!

Before I end this chapter, let's talk about a man's ticking clock. He doesn't have one. A man can plant his seed pretty much up until he's dead. This is another biological, instinctual and natural reason men have a different view of marriage than women.

Yet, there IS a ticking clock. A lot of men in their 30's start to wonder what it will be like for them when they do have kids. They're thinking, "I'm afraid I'm going to be too old to play ball with my son. He'll be 15 when I'm 50!"

Knowing this, don't pressure a man by constantly talking about how much you want to have kids. *REVERSE the process*. Subtly plant seeds. Have a picnic at a park where you know fathers and sons will be playing ball. (Perhaps, you can get him there by telling him you're making a fantastic picnic lunch. Hey, just a thought.) Or how about renting one of your favorite movies that just happens to be 'The Bad News Bears'? (The original, not the remake.)

While you guys are watching it, you can say something like, "I feel bad for Walter Matthau."

In between stuffing popcorn and nachos into his mouth, he'll grunt "Huh? Why?"

170

You'll answer, "He seems so lonely. Well, not when he's playing ball with the kids. But he looks old. He can barely keep up with them."

Plant seeds like this and his maternal instincts, check that—his male ego will come out and perhaps, he will want to spread his seed in one garden. Yours. Ya' know, the Garden of Eden. Paradise. A place no one wants to ever leave.

POINT VALUE: Plus ten for you personally if you get him to say, "Honey, how you would feel about starting a family?"

FOR THE SIX MEN READING THIS BOOK: Do you really want to get used to hearing (if you can still hear, that is), some kid saying to your kid, "Your grandfather is here to take you home."

I Can Tell You, but Then You'd Have to Kill Me

> Men Lack Tact. If You're Going to Ask a Question Like, "Do You Think I Look Fat in This Dress," Don't Get Mad When He Says, "Yes." You Asked.

When a group of kids were asked how they would make a marriage work, Rickey, age 10 said, *"Tell your wife that she looks pretty, even if she looks like a truck"*
– Ten-year-old boy who is smarter than most grown men

SOMETIMES, men don't think. Okay, okay. Many times, men don't think. We don't always realize that when you ask certain questions like, "How do I look in this dress?" or "Do you like my new haircut?" or "Do you think my butt looks big in this outfit?" What you really want is reassurance. Mr. Knuckle-dragger gives the wrong answer, you get mad at him, and now he's confused because he thought you really wanted to know his opinion.

Even the knuckle-draggers, who are smart enough to give reassurance, get into a Catch-22 more times than not. It's **very** frustrating. Let's say he doesn't like that dress, but he says, "I love that dress, Honey," but he doesn't say it with enough conviction, so you say, "I know you're lying" and he's dumb enough to say, "Okay, well, I'm not a big fan of it." Now, you're hurt, and he gets into trouble.

I was dating Diane. She felt like she had put on a few pounds. She had. She asked me. I said I hadn't noticed any difference. She kept pressing the issue, so I got stupid and said something like, "Maybe a few." I spent the rest of the evening telling her she looked beautiful, she spent the rest of the evening saying, "You think I'm fat!"

AHHHHHHHHHHHHHHH!!!

POINT VALUE: Minus three if you press us for an answer, then get mad when Mr. Dumbass gives you one you didn't want to hear.

FOR THE SIX MEN READING THIS BOOK: (A) If you feel your woman needs to lose weight, I suggest you look at your flabby-self before you say something stupid. (B) When she asks a question like that, your job is to reassure your woman and make her feel good about herself. Ya' know, like when you ask her if she came. Do you really want to know all that "Oh God, yes, oh Goddddddd, yessssss!!!!!!!!!!" was an act?

Peanuts Land

Don't Talk on and on. Keep Your
Conversations Short and Concise

"I was gratified to be able to answer promptly. I said I don't know."

– Mark Twain

WE men love, love, love to hear ourselves speak... when we're talking about ourselves. We'll go into details, tell grand stories, use big words, think we're all that and more!

However, when it comes to other subjects, especially subjects that aren't 'manly', or ones that have to do with relationship 'stuff', men think of it as 'stuff'—we would rather not talk about that stuff. If you don't give short answers and go into long details—men will smile or nod or say, "Yes dear", or "Uh huh" or "Wow!" But what he's hearing is: "Wa, wa, wa, wa, wa," like when adults speak in Peanuts cartoons.

Okay, okay, not all men hear "Wa, wa, wa, wa, wa". Some of us hear "Blah, blah, blah, blah, blah." It's not okay that we do it, but we do it. (I know women do this to men too—but again, this book is about understanding him.) Try to keep it brief. Or as I like to say to my sisters when they go into what are truly unnecessary details: 'Land the plane'. If you learn how to land the plane—you are that much closer to landing the man.

Here are some great answers that work for many questions: 'Yes'. 'No'. 'Sure'. '8:00'. 'Next week'. 'At Monica's house'. Got it? Okay. Good!

SUBCONSCIOUS POINT VALUE: Plus eight if the answers are short and sweet.
Six minus if you don't see the glazed look and keep on and on.

FOR THE SIX MEN READING THIS BOOK: If she goes into more details than you think are necessary, don't get angry. Gently say, 'Land the plane'. If she really wants to go into details, let her, maybe they are more important than you realize. I know, I know…

O.C.D. and A.D.D. It Up

"In youth we learn; in age we understand."
— Marie Ebner-Eschenbach
(Born Countess Dubsky, she is considered one of the most important German-language writers of the latter portion of the 19th century.)

WE men all have some form of O.C.D. (Obsessive Compulsive Disorder) and A.D.D. (Attention Deficit Disorder). It's how we're built. We fixate on something—then lose interest. A man's A.D.D., especially when it comes to women, is stronger than his O.C.D., so you want to score points, so he fixates on you and does not lose interest in you.

Another reason we need to control the clicker is that while channel surfing, if we stay on something we don't want to watch for more than a second and a half, we get all tense and jittery.

If you want to talk to your man about something important and *you want his full attention*, say to him; "I need your undivided attention. When can we talk?" Then mutually find a time. He will appreciate that you understand him. You will appreciate that he'll be listening, and not hearing, "Wa wa, wa wa."

How do you get a man's undivided attention? Obviously, TV off, Xbox off, anything distracting gone. Then, sit across from him and talk to him using words with no more than one syllable. Okay, once again, I exaggerate to make a point. A bit. A tiny bit.

Perhaps you can have this conversation over some tasty treat you made for him. You'll have his attention, and he'll be more vulnerable because his tummy feels so good and warm and happy and you're the one who made his tummy feel so good and warm and happy. Triple/Double.

A place I am going to suggest you talk to him is going to sound a little contradictory, but here goes: Take him to a baseball game. I find that when my friends and I go to a baseball game, besides eating a lot of bad food, we talk a lot.

There's a reason baseball has a Seventh Inning Stretch.[10] Baseball isn't exactly action packed. This is the reason you hear announcers talk on and on about statistics. They need to fill the gaps. They don't need to land the plane.

When he's at a baseball game, he doesn't have the benefit of a gap-filling announcer—*something he's used to*—something that has become a habit for him because of when he watches baseball on TV. At a game, he's confused and befuddled. He doesn't know what to do. So, he talks. If you go with him, you can be the one filling those gaps.

Now, be prepared to talk… cheer… talk/cheer… talk… moan… talk… yawn… talk/cheer… high-five strangers… recap what just happened with friends and strangers… talk… commiserate with friends and strangers… and possibly, even get frustrated because the line to the men's room is about ten deep and the one to the ladies' room is around the block.

The conversation might be a bit more sporadic than you'd like, but he might actually be listening between those three exciting plays.

SUBCONSCIOUS POINT VALUE: Plus five because you're not trying to have an important conversation with him while he's doing something that he wants to focus on.

FOR THE SIX MEN READING THIS BOOK: If she asks for your undivided attention, give it to her. She has something important she needs to say. If you don't understand why it's so important, try to read between the lines 'cause she might just be saying, "I need more attention from you."

---

[10] The seventh inning stretch occurs in the middle of the seventh inning. After the away team finishes their half of the inning and before the home team comes to the plate, the fans get up, stretch, and sing "Take me out to the ball game"—which makes no sense since they're already at the ball game.

Jell-O Puddin'

> Unwarranted Jealousy Will Kill Your
> Relationship

"Pain is inevitable. Suffering is optional."
— M. Kathleen Casey (Writer and Artist)

SOME say 'trust' is the cornerstone of a relationship. I say it's the cornerstone, the side-stone, the front-stone, and all the stones in the foundation because, as I said, without trust, there is no 'us'. Without trust, a relationship can never really move forward, and it certainly can't be a happy and healthy one for either party. Why get jealous over things there are no reasons to get jealous over? You will lose MAJOR points and it will kill your relationship.

Treat your man like Jell-O. Huh?

Take a cube of Jell-O and put it in the palm of your open hand. Go on and do it, it's fun. Now, hold onto it tightly.

Okay, stop. I can see you're still reading and not doing it. I'll wait. *Dooo doo doo doo doo*. That's me humming while I wait, something most of us rarely do, but it seems many people in movies do, *doo doo doo dooooooooo*.

Okay, enough doo dooo doooing. If you didn't do it now, next chance you get to hold Jell-O, give it a try and stop worrying that everyone in the cafeteria or that party thinks you've lost it. Be a kid every now and then. Put the cube of Jell-O into your open hand—then hold onto it really tight. Squeeze your hand into a tight fist. What happens? The Jell-O seeps out. Now, place another piece of Jell-O in the palm of your open hand. Keep your hand open and run around with the Jell-O in it. What happens? It stays put.

Men are like Jell-O. If you try to hold onto us too tight, we feel caged and will 'seep out'. If you hold us in an open palm, we can stay in your hands forever.

I was dating this woman, Joanna. Liked her a lot. Things were going well for the first few months. Not long, but long enough to know I wanted to see how far this could go. One day, Joanna finds these matches in my desk drawer. In them is a woman's name and phone number. Joanna assumes:

WOMAN'S NAME + NUMBER ON MATCHBOOK = I'M UP TO NO GOOD!!!

She goes ballistic. I can't get a word in edgewise. Finally, I said, "Are you done?"

She wasn't, but I was. So I shouted, "THE MATCHBOOK IS LIKE THREE YEARS OLD!"

And what does Joanna say? Come on, ladies, you know what she said. "If you didn't care about her anymore, you would have thrown it out!" (You ladies have a knowing smile, don't you?)

Throw it out? I didn't even know 'it' still existed! It was in a drawer with other 'it' junk.

I told Joanna, "I don't remember if I ever even called Ms. Matchbook."

I couldn't remember, which should have also been a signal to Joanna that Ms. Matchbook obviously didn't make any kind of long-lasting impression on me and this conversation should end.

Nope, the conversation did not end.

"You wouldn't have taken the matches from her in the first place if you didn't want to be with her."

I stood there—not sure if I blinked. I was amazed at this non-logic. Sure, maybe three years ago I was interested in going on a date with Ms. Matchbook, but that was THREE YEARS AGO.

I wanted to try to make things work with Joanna because when we first met she was a 'nine' on a scale of one to ten. So I let it go. But this kind of needless jealousy reared its ugly head too often. So by the time I ended it, Joanna was a minus two.

Obviously, Joanna's jealousy had nothing to do with numbers on a matchbook. It had to do with a fundamental distrust she had. A fundamental distrust in men that many women have—rightfully so.

This distrust exists because:

1   Some women will prosecute a man for who they used to be, not who they are with them.
2   You've been hurt too many times in the past by some guy you trusted who broke your trust and your heart. Sometimes it's a man you've dated. Sometimes it's the father who left. It's a painful fire that burns deep and isn't helped by the fact that gasoline is often poured on it because of—
3   W.O.E. (Don't kill the messenger.)

As Joanna and I got closer, she got worried she'd lose me. She tightened her grip—and she lost me. "What we fear most will come to be?"

Jell-O, ladies, Jell-O. Why? There is nothing you can do to stop a man who is bent on cheating, but you can lose a man by not trusting ones who won't. This kind of jealousy makes a man feel like he's in jail and you're the jailor. He will feel caged and then feel the need to break out of this cage. This kind of jealousy will not only lose you points but will push him to cheat. If you treat someone like a criminal, they are going to become a criminal.

You've heard that "jealousy is a wasted emotion," but you've rarely heard why. It's because it not only wastes time and energy, it can lay to waste what might have been a great relationship—if it was given a chance.

When I dated Alice, I thought she was the one. The chemistry was on fire, we had many of the same interests, we laughed together, etc. But as Alice and I grew closer, she started to tighten her grip and well, Wonderland wasn't looking so good. She tightened her grip because she started to get jealous of my background. She distrusted me because of past issues in her life, and because I had not been landed by any other woman. She figured I was going to take off on her. I can't fight the past, so I tried very hard to show Alice how much I loved her and how much I wanted this to work. Nothing worked. I was constantly questioned, and/or accused, about this or that. Her fist was closing and the Jell-O (me) was seeping out. I got so much grief, I ended up doing what she feared most. I cheated on her.

I figured, "Well, if she's gonna be this way and I haven't done anything, I might as well have a little fun before I get the grief that's coming my way, no matter what I do or don't do!"

I am not proud of this and would rather not be telling you. But I promised you I would be honest to help you learn about us men. I should have 'been a man' and broken up with her before I went elsewhere because, at that point, I was looking for a way out of the cage she had created through jealousy. Consequently, because of that unnecessary and uncalled for jealousy, what might have been a great relationship never stood a chance.

Another reason we get jealous is that we fear that by losing someone, we are also losing ourselves. Many women can and tend to lose themselves and their identity to the guy they are dating. You are not defined by the man you are with. There are countless things that define you. I believe what most defines a person is how they treat others, and how they act, especially during times of great achievement as well as the low times in their lives.

I have seen too many relationships, ones that had so much going for them, end over needless jealousy.

Yes, a little jealousy here and there is not a bad thing because we all want to feel wanted. But when it's constant and constantly over nothing, it gets tiring, frustrating and it will kill the relationship, nail the coffin, bada-bing, the gate closed, and forget about it ever working out. Who wants to defend themselves all the time for things they didn't do?

If there is a reason to be jealous, that's another story, a story that should quickly end by you closing that book, tossing him back into the toad pond then fishing for a better book in a different pond.

If you're with a man you can't trust because you really shouldn't trust him—please close this book, turn it to the front and smack yourself in the head with it. Maybe, that will knock some sense into you and you'll move on to a better man.

I am not a woman so I wouldn't dare tell you how to overcome needless jealousy. I will tell you that, if you have studied his patterns, you know if you have any reason to be jealous, trust that you have done your homework well, and use your innate powers of perception and your Sixth Sense and you'll know. Most of the time, you ladies really know when there is a real reason to be upset. I believe women are born with a radar system that would make every spy satellite in space look like they were built by some kid using his Lego toy set. Use that 'satellite' system of yours before you leap.

While you're at it, why not make him some Jell-O Puddin'? He'll enjoy that you made him something, and you can have a little knowing smile and reminder to yourself.

SUBCONSCIOUS POINT VALUE: Plus ten if you show him that you trust him.

Minus ten if you consistently get jealous over things that you really shouldn't.

FOR THE SIX MEN READING THIS BOOK: By nature, you're a dawg. By nature, other women could care less if you're dating or even married if she considers you a good catch. Your woman has her reasons to have her guard up, so do whatever you can, whenever you can, to make her feel secure about you and your relationship.

Am I a Clown, Here to Amuse You?

We Love Being Around People We Can Laugh With

"Among those whom I like or admire, I can find no common denominator, but among those whom I love, I can: all of them make me laugh."

– W. H. Auden
(Considered by many to be the greatest English poet of the 20th Century)

STUDIES show that laughter can heal many illnesses. No one knows for sure why. Maybe it's because we're taking in a lot of oxygen when we laugh. Maybe it's because it fills our hearts with hope and joy and we want to stay around because we feel so hopeful and joyous. Maybe it's because it makes us realize that life, with all its sadness, is worth living. Whatever the reason, we all want laughter in our lives. Without it, the world would be a much emptier, darker place.

Whenever I've dated a woman who didn't share my sense of humor, it didn't last very long. She didn't have to be funny, but I really enjoyed it when she enjoyed me being funny. Sure, there were times I'd say something I thought was funny and get nothing in response. I might even get an eye-roll. But if, for the most part, she couldn't laugh with me or get me to laugh, a big piece of the relationship pie was missing, and it was not a piece I could do without. I would move on.

Most men feel this way. Who needs someone in their life that rains a dark cloud on, what to them, is a funny moment? Laughter is a common bond. It is a glue that can hold together the worst of situations.

You can't be taught to have a sense of humor, so if you're with someone who doesn't find much funny about anything, and you're a person who loves to laugh, it's not going to work.

POINT VALUE: Plus ten if you both can enjoy moments of laughter together. Beyond plus ten if you can find humor in situations that are less than perfect.

500 BONUS POINTS if you know what movie "Am I a clown here to amuse you?" is from. As I said, we men love to quote movies! FYI: Nothing wrong with using Google and other technology to your advantage. It's an easy, quick way to gain points and an advantage over the competition.)

FOR THE SIX MEN READING THIS BOOK: Ditto. (Except the bonus points. You don't get that for the easy stuff like knowing every line from 'Caddyshack', 'Ghostbusters' and Star Wars; Episodes one through eight.) You get those bonus points for knowing the hard stuff like her birthday or the day you started dating her. Yes, I said 'Or'. We really can't be expected to remember both. What do we look like, geniuses?

Even King Kong Felt Pain

He's More Sensitive Than You Think. Do What
You Can to Protect His Feelings

*"I'd much rather be a woman than a man. Women can cry,
they can wear cute clothes, and they're the first to be
rescued off sinking ships."*
– Gilda Radner,
(Brilliant sketch comedian and
actor who left us too soon

MEN have huge egos. This is why men are more sensitive and insecure than women. Yes, I said men are more sensitive and insecure than women. Something no man likes to talk about, let alone admit, even to himself.

Men feel the need to prove so many things so much of the time. Men want to outsmart, out do, out earn, run, throw, punch, and fuck every other man out there. If that's not insecurity, I don't know what is.

We are especially sensitive and insecure when it comes to winning over a woman and keeping a woman won over. You can and should use this to your advantage by doing all you can to stroke his ego, and all you can to not bruise it.

The reason men's egos are so fragile is that we know we're full of crap. We know that a lot of what we beat our chests about is hot air and show—and beneath it all is an unsure, sometimes scared little boy. And NO MAN wants that to be revealed. Thus, we overcompensate.

Where there is ego and insecurity, sensitivity is sure to follow. Many women make the mistake of not realizing how sensitive men are, and sometimes say or do things that can hurt us more than you know. Or things happen in our lives that we 'shrug off', so you don't think we need you to be there

185

for us. We do. On our terms, of course, which are hard to gauge because many times we not only don't tell you we're hurting, but we also want our space. Women change their minds a lot; men want you there for us and our space. Both sexes have their idiosyncrasies.

It's not your fault when you don't realize your man is hurting, because most men aren't going to say, "I'm feeling hurt," or "You hurt my feelings." We're going to suck it in and take it like a man! How can you figure out how, or if your man is hurting? You got it! You've studied his patterns; you see the way he is. Handle him right and he will feel you truly understand him and are there for him when he needs you—as well as when he wants to keep to himself.

As you know, I grew up with three sisters. I watched them, along with my mother, get emotional over many different things and tried my best to help them through it all. They cried, I didn't. They showed their pain, I sucked mine in. I had some tough situations growing up; I never showed that it got to me. I had to deal with family issues at a young age, and I did so 'like a man'.

I got into some fights protecting their virtue. I lost some fights protecting their virtue. Still no tears. I only cried twice growing up. Once, when my dog was hit by a car and died. The other time was when my other dog had to be put down. Both times I sucked it in and 'took it like a man'. Then, I left the room and, when no one could see me, I let it out.

No one ever taught me "men don't cry?" No one ever said to me, "Take it like a man." *It was instinctual.*

That's why men's egos are so huge. Way back in Cave Town, we needed huge egos to face our fears or we wouldn't have survived.

All animals sense emotions. Those in the wild just seem more attuned. We especially sense pain and fear because an animal with those emotions is easier prey. Men had to hunt in order to eat in order to survive. Man was prey for some of the animals he hunted. The last thing he wanted was that animal to sense fear, pain or anything but confidence and strength. Ego building was essential. If one's ego wasn't massive, one is not going to leave the cave. Yes, women needed ego as well. But men provided while women nurtured, so men built up their egos to make them larger than life to step out of that cave and fight whatever life was throwing at them.

Another reason I believe men have bigger egos than women is that women are more in tune with their instincts. Women trust their inner strength more than men do. I never lived in Cave Town. When I became a writer, I became more in touch with my feminine side and more open with my emotions. Yet, to this day, I still feel the need in many, many situations, to not show and tell.

Pitching for my softball team, I got slammed in the jaw with the ball—and still made the throw to first after I hit the ground. I didn't go to the emergency room because "I can take it like a man!" The next day the doctor told me that my jaw was broken—in two places! My jaw got wired shut. Then when it came time for the doctor to remove the wires, I was in serious pain. He was shaking his head while he worked.

He was about halfway done with the top half of my mouth when he said, in amazement, "No one has ever refused anesthesia before!"

What? Huh? What? My mind, through the intense pain, raced back. He DID ask me something before we started, and I misunderstood him. Why didn't he ask again? What idiot would refuse anesthesia? Apparently, me. I'm about to say something like, "Give me the anesthesia!" when he says, "I'm going to have to write about this and send it to the New England Journal of Medicine." Now, there's no way I'm going to say anything because now, I'm a man who can 'take it like a man' in front of a man who is amazed at my manliness and is going to write about my manliness and all men will see how manly a man I am! Mind you, he had the rest of the top to do and the entire bottom.

Did I 'suck it in' because I'm an idiot? Yes! Am I this kind of idiot because I'm a man and want to be able to 'take it like a man?' Yes!

That was physical pain. Imagine how much harder it is for a man to show emotional pain.

Most men are more guarded than most women, so when a man really falls in love, it's beyond deep. When he's dumped, his pain is also beyond deep, it is to be hidden and never to be discussed. If you don't believe a man has a harder time recuperating from love lost, why is it that studies show in a long marriage when the wife dies, the husband is soon to follow? When a husband dies, the reverse is not true.

If your man is hurt or you've hurt your man's feelings, there's a chance you won't even know it. Use what you've learned by studying his patterns and your innate powers of perception to empower yourself and be sensitive to the fact that even King Kong felt pain.

SUBCONSCIOUS POINT VALUE: Plus nine and a half when you're there for him, even if that means giving him his space and saying nothing. Plus nine when you stroke his ego and make him feel like he can 'take it like a man!'

FOR THE SIX MEN READING THIS BOOK: Sometimes, strike that, many times you're a tactless idiot-face. Cut your woman some slack if she says something that hurts your feelings. Give her the benefit of the doubt that whatever it is that she said was not on purpose. She's 'in your corner'.[11]

---

[11] Boxers have a 'Corner Man." They wait outside the boxers' corner until a round ends, then they step into the corner and help out their boxer. Without a good corner man, the boxer would lose. Angelo Dundee, Muhammad Ali's long time corner man, is considered one of the greatest.

Your Friendly Neighborhood Spider-Man

> Let Your Man Do "Manly" Things. But Don't
> Be Too Needy

"A woman is like a tea bag: you can't tell how strong she is until you put her on hot water"
— Eleanor Roosevelt
(Champion of the underprivileged.
She transformed the role of First Lady from
serving tea to dishing out political wisdom.)

IF the man you want is a take-charge kinda guy, why not let him? Men like to feel like men. Men like to do 'manly' things, like open doors for you, give meaningless advice—control the TV remote! These are manly things for manly men that make us feel like manly superheroes.

That being said, most men would rather be lovers than fighters. Hopefully, you're with this kind of a man. Don't get him into a fight by mouthing off to some guy when you're with your man. (For that matter, don't do it when you're not. There are a lot of people full of rage and you don't want it directed at you.) As much as your man wants to be, he ain't Spidey and someone could get hurt or worse.

I'm out to dinner with Crystal. It's a first date. She's an eight. We take a walk in an area where there are lots of restaurants and bars. NOT a residential neighborhood. Not that I'm sure that matters, but you'll see where I'm going with this in a sec. Some guys drive by in their truck—music blasting. She yells something like, "Hey, asshole, turn down your music!" When their tires screeched to a halt and they zoomed backwards towards us, guess who had to deal with it?

Crystal went from an eight to a minus 50, and I was lucky I didn't have my head bashed in.

When it comes to less violent issues, most men still want to be the rescuer, yet want to know his woman can do for yourself, unless you discover your man likes being the caretaker and needs to feel you'd be lost without him. Caretakers, however, usually move on to take care of another because (A) they feel the person they are with is either fixed and/or doesn't need them anymore or (B) they find another who needs to be taken care of even more.

Most men want women who aren't needy, yet need him for certain things. Things that make him feel like a manly superhero!

At one point in my life, I was a caretaker. I would move on when 'my job' was done. Having realized what I was doing, having figured out something was lacking inside of me and it was that which I sought, I changed my patterns. I realized we are all outsiders looking in—and many of us feel unworthy. I decided it was time to feel worthy and date a woman I could be a superhero with but not have to rescue all the time. By this, I mean a woman who can have what she desires in life without depending on someone else to achieve those desires, yet knows when to let me help, let me be a superhero—let me be a man.

This "I want to save you but I want you to be able to swim" might sound like a bit of a contradiction, and it is, but they really do work together because sometimes contradictions make sense.

"What you just said is another contradiction, Mr. Knuckle-dragger." True, so is the phrase, 'Opposites attract'.

My point is you know when you're being too needy and when to let a man feel like a manly superhero. Use this to your advantage. Let him feel like a superhero when you walk into a restaurant and he wants to be the one to say, "Reservation for two under Mr. Spider-Man!" Let him save your life by opening up that jelly jar. Let him protect you by letting him mansplain and give you dumb advice—you don't have to listen. Let him shield you from dangerous flames of fire and barbecue the meat.

Why not Tom Sawyer your Spider-Man so he does things for you around the house. Not only will he feel like a hero, not only will you get things fixed, he'll also be around you and get more and more used to being around you; thus, forming a habit. Double/Triple!

Look at all the fairy tales we grew up with. The prince rescues the damsel in distress. Fairy tales like "Frozen" have thankfully changed the dynamic in fairy tales BUT the "We must save you, Woman" attitude is still within most men. In most fairy tales men are the heroes and women get everlasting true love. Thus, the term "Fairy tale." We men think when we're manly men, we're superheroes (the modern-day version of a prince coming to the princess's rescue. This is something we men want to feel, have to feel and *need to feel* in order to feel like men.

So, let him feel it. Let him be your knight in shining armor.

I just realized something, or consciously realized something, I want to share with you. I am, despite all the disappointments, a romantic. I hope you are as well. I hope you realize that you should never settle for less. I still, still believe fairy tales can come true. But what I've just come to realize is that to really be a superhero in a relationship, the evildoers you need to defeat and the demons you must outsmart are not the ones on the road to 'saving' the princess. They are the ones on the road you travel together, as prince and princess, as man and woman—as husband and wife.

POINT VALUE: Plus six if you let him be (or at least think he is) your superhero.

Minus seven if he wants to be Spider-Man, but Wonder Woman keeps beating him to the punch.

FOR THE SIX MEN READING THIS BOOK: I want to repeat something I just wrote:

The evildoers you need to defeat and the demons you must outsmart are not the ones on the road to 'saving' the princess. They are the ones on the road you travel TOGETHER, as prince and princess, as man and woman—as husband and wife.

Also, if I had my choice, chivalry would be back into style. Yes, I know you women don't need a man to do any of these things for you. But I think there's something nice about it. Something—romantic. I like opening doors for a woman. I like to carry the packages, pull out her chair, walk her to her door, and stand when she enters the room. (Be prepared to have everyone look at you like your crazy when you do this one, especially if you're at a restaurant with a group of women. There will be lots of standing and sitting. If you're not doing some of these things for your woman, you're not Spider-Man… you're The Green Goblin.

Don Juan Demarco

Help Your Man to Feel Secure about Himself
and It Will Help Him Feel Secure About
Being With You

*"Sex appeal is fifty percent what you've got and fifty percent
what people think you've got"*
— Sophia Loren
(Actor, singer, writer, mother, legend)

ALL men think they're Don Juan. <u>ALL</u> men. Don't believe
me? Look at many of the shows on TV. You know, the ones
where the overweight, balding, not too good-looking guy,
who doesn't have the greatest personality, doesn't make much
money and doesn't have much of a brain is married to a sexy,
beautiful, smart woman. By the way, who do you think
created those shows, women or men? And take a guess what
most of those men look like.

Although men think they are Don Juan, they know they're
not. Here's where you come in. You love compliments. We
love compliments. As I said, we men are more insecure than
you think, and we are more insecure than you. We want our
bodies to look good, our status in life to mean something, our
hair to stay on our heads and off our backs, our performance
in bed to be stupendous and a host of other things that make
our woman think we're the best at everything we do.

Help your man to feel secure, boost his ego—score huge
points.

Flattery will get you everywhere. Tell your man great
things about himself. If you can't think of any, why are you
with Mr. I-Have-Nothing-Good-To-Say-About-You? Tell
your man how great he looks. How great he makes you feel.

How lucky you are to be with him… all the things you love to hear from him. Did I mention men are more insecure than women and flattery WILL get you everywhere… including his heart?

One of the most important things to compliment your man on is, yep, you know, how great he is in bed. You ladies know this one because that's why the 'Fake Orgasm' was invented.

"Oh, yes, yes yesssaaaaaa!!!"

It makes a man feel good to hear that, so you fake it. I would guess you fake it not only to make him feel good about himself but to get him off you, so he'll fall asleep and you can find someone who knows how to satisfy you. You.

Say to your man, "You're amazing in bed! You're Don Juan DeMarco!!" He's not going to question it. He might say, 'Really?' But once you reassure him, he's not going to question it… until the next time the two of you make love or have sex.

Okay, what if he needs improvement in this area? What if his last girlfriend loved it when he used his little finger and went clockwise really fast and you like it when he uses his thumb and goes counter-clockwise really slow. Say something during the act, while moaning; "Oh, Honey, that's sooo good, Ohhhhh yessss, that's it, ohhhh… think you can you use your chin a little more? Ohhhhhh."

What if he just plain sucks in bed? How about leaving magazines in the bathroom with articles like, "How men can be great lovers" or "How to please your woman like never before" or "The Female Orgasm: Myth or Fact? Fact."

Maybe, you can get a porno and watch it together. Say, "I'd like to try that" if you'd like to try that.

Whatever tactic you use—magazines, porn, or a heartfelt conversation through moaning—you owe it to yourself and your relationship to do something to have a great sex life. Because no one should ever have to suffer like that, even if it is only for two, maybe two and a half minutes.

POINT VALUE: Plus ten if you make him feel like Don Juan. Minus ten if you make him feel less like Don Juan and more like Elmer J. Fudd. Nothing personal, Elmer.

FOR THE SIX MEN READING THIS BOOK: Do I really need to tell you to make sure your woman feels like a

Goddess? To make sure she knows she's the sexiest woman alive? That sincere compliments are the most important gift you can give to her? Of course, I do! 'Cause you're a freakin' idiot.

Body Double

*"Men always want to be a woman's first love. Women like to
be a man's last romance."*
— Oscar Wilde
(Legendary Irish poet and dramatist. Wrote, 'The
Importance of Being Earnest' and 'The Picture of Dorian
Gray')

Don't tell your man what another man has said about you
sexually. If your man says, "I like the way you kiss," don't
say, "I've been told I'm a great kisser." If he says, "I like the
way you taste," don't say, "I know, my last boyfriend said I
tasted like candy!" If you do, your man is wondering if you
still think about this Mr. Other Dick and how often.

Many times, it's not as much a jealousy thing as it is a
territory thing. I know a woman isn't 'territory'. But I also
know how men think and we men think of you as ours. All
the political correctness isn't going to change this. (Men
won't admit it as much, that's all that will change). Not ours
to do with what we want. Ours in that, you are his women and
not another man's.

So, when he gives you a compliment like, "Honey, you're
a great kisser, say, "Thank you." Or better still, "That's
because you're such a great kisser."

Whatever you do, don't tell him how many other men
you've had sex with. I know you already know this, but you
know how I like to repeat basics.

If and when that subject comes up (and oral sex counts
ladies), lie. Most men really don't want to know the truth
about your past sexual experiences, even if he asks. This is

the only thing I am going to tell you to blatantly lie about. It's not playing a game when you are protecting another person's feelings and yes, you are protecting his feelings because he doesn't need to know how many men you've slept with. It has no effect on your present relationship. It's the past. The man you want is the present and hopefully future.

It's like you asking your man what he thinks of your dress, shoes, hair, hips, nose, weight, etc. Do you really want to know how he feels, or do you want his reassurance?

A man who sleeps with a lot of women is called a stud. A woman who sleeps with a lot of men is known by many terms, none of which you want him to associate with you. Yes, it's a double standard. Yes, it's not fair. Yes, it's sexist. But it exists. You can fight windmills or lie. Lie.

A man wants your reassurance that his 'territory' hasn't been invaded too often. All men want a woman who can be the MVP on his team. Most men don't want a woman who happens to be with the entire team.

POINT VALUE: Plus five if whatever the truth is, you keep the number in his comfort zone. Minus seven if you feel the need to kiss and tell, and that number is beyond something he's comfortable with.

FOR THE SIX MEN READING THIS BOOK: 1. She's with you now. If you're worried she's going to go back to Mr. Other Dick, perhaps you should study her patterns to see if you two are on the same path. 2. So what if you find out she has slept with more guys than you would have liked? As long as you're the only guy she's sleeping with now, why care? And who are you to judge anyway?! There's a good chance that you've slept with your fair share of women. If she happens to beat you in this area, consider yourself lucky that she wants you because she has tested the waters and chose you to be the permanent dip in her pool.

Johnny Rocket

> True or Not, Let Your Man Know His Penis Is the Best Penis You've Ever Had.

"You will do foolish things, so do them with enthusiasm."
— Colette
(French novelist who wrote over 50 novels. Known for her themes on female sexuality in the male-dominated world.)

THE penis. We men have them. We men use them. We men name them. Penises are different than vaginas. I don't know many women who name their vajaja. Okay, vajaja is a name, but it's different. That's just a nickname because for some women, saying vagina in mixed company, can be a little uncomfortable (I do not know why). Men, however, are not uncomfortable talking about our Willy Wonka in any company. (Some men are so not uncomfortable about their penis they send pictures of him to women who don't ask for them. This kind of men are called, "Fuckturds" and these kinds of men, unless you're looking for a bedroom relationship only are to be avoided, and in some cases, put in prison. Yes, that's another book).

So here is my theory as to why men name their Johnson. First of all, the word 'penis' doesn't sound very strong, tough, or warrior-like. It sounds kinda meek and weak. No way can something so mighty be meek and weak. So, we use stronger, more powerful words.

The other reason we name our Jack Johnson is so we can talk about 'him' in the third person. If Johnny Rocket is someone else, we can blame him when we do something stupid.

"It wasn't my fault! It was Rocket's!"

In our heads, both of them, actually, gives us an excuse, and we all know a very poor one at that, as to why we do some of the dumbass things we do. As long as he has a name, we can say Dick Slippery is a living, thinking, all-powerful entity that works independently of us. He's the real bearer of our sins.

"I wouldn't have done it if Apollo eight and a half hadn't made me!"

How and when we start to name our Italian Stallone, I'm not really sure. This is a long-standing tradition (excuse the pun), among men not dared to be broken, for the ramifications could be disastrous.

A friend of mine, Adriana, who has an eleven-year-old son, said, "I've read tons of books on parenting and they tell you to call body parts by their medical names when you're with your kids. But, little boys will still insist on calling it everything but its medical name and have many, many different names for it. It starts at an early age."

She went on to tell me her son has many names for his Jack Nicholson. I asked, how did he know to name him?

She said, "Who knows. Maybe his father, friends, TV…"

"What does any of this have to do with us getting a man, Mr. Knuckle-dragger?"

I'm glad you asked.

We want Happy Harry to be the greatest, you've ever met. We don't want another man's Fred Flintstone to have been better than our Empire State Building. So don't talk about another man's Richard Nixon (a fine name for a penis if it's a little crooked), unless for some strange reason your man asks. Then say, "Oscar Mayer is the mightiest and best ever!"

Remember—his ego is fragile. Your man wants to feel safe with you, in all aspects of life, including, and possibly especially, when it comes to how you feel about his Obi Wan Kenobi.

POINT VALUE: Plus ten for making your man feel like he has the best Johnny Johnson ever. Minus eight if you talk about another man and his sexual prowess.

FOR YOU SIX MEN READING THE BOOK:

1. Saying, "It was Mr. Ollivander Phoenix Feather Wand's fault!" fault!" doesn't cut it and you know it. "Be a man," or more like most women and take responsibility when you mess up. Not just with your woman, with anything. Don't be like a typical politician who passes the blame onto everyone else.

Be a stand-up guy who says, "I take full responsibility. The buck stops here!"

I hate when people play the victim or the blame game (That's yet another book).

2. Numbnuts, don't talk about other women you've slept with to your woman!

Don't say, "My last girlfriend had huge jugs!" We all know we're idiots and say idiot things but try—TRY—to refrain from speaking before thinking. Then once you think—stay quiet. Your mind is not your friend.

3. Studies show if you buy a Hummer, monster truck, or any red sports car, your One Eyed Pirate will automatically lose two inches the moment you drive off the lot.

Second Time Around

What Divorced Women Should Do and Not Do in Order to Get a New Man

"You may encounter many defeats, but you must not be defeated. In fact, it may be necessary to encounter the defeats, so you can know who you are, what you can rise from, how you can still come out of it.
– Maya Angelou
(One of the greatest and boldest American poets and civil rights activist ever to grace our world)

YOU want another chance, and you most certainly deserve another chance to find the right man to marry. Maybe your ex-husband was the right man and it just took its course. Maybe he was Mr. All Wrong. Whatever the reason you have for having an ex-husband if when you meet a man you like enough to want to marry, try not to talk about your ex. (This goes for ex-boyfriends as well). Don't trash your ex—too much or too often.

"Thou doth protest too much," he mayeth thinketh.

I dated this woman, Eva, and really liked her a lot. She was a seven and a half on my yellow pad. A couple of months into what I hoped would go a lot longer; she trashed her ex who she dated for seven years. This happened several other times. I figured she was still in love because she still had this deep hate for him, so my wall went way up, and I kept her at arm's length because the foundation of our relationship— trust—cracked.

Mr. NewMan must feel 100% that you and Mr. Ex are over. You could be friends with your ex and that's fine as long as you make your new man feel comfortable with it. If Mr.

NewMan refuses to meet your ex and be comfortable with him, perhaps you should get a Mr. NewNewMan.

If you're not over Mr. Ex, go out and have fun, but don't be out there looking to get married. You'll make a bad decision... again. Let your wounds heal. Sure, put Mr. Band-Aid on them for a while, and then peel him off, let your wounds really heal and move on with your life.

Present pain is tolerable IF you realize you have a future. And you always, always have a future. Every new second presents a new future and a world of new opportunities.

It just happened. Oh, there it goes again. Oh, there was another future.

It doesn't matter if your marriage (or relationship) has been over for ten minutes or ten years. Mr. NewMan, the man you want now, is on guard and his wall is up with turrets and a moat until he knows for sure it's over.

If Mr. NewMan brings up your ex, if he asks any questions, don't flinch. Tell Mr. NewMan (ya know, the guy with the fragile ego), that he's better at everything than Mr. Ex. Again, this might not be totally true, but you're not playing a game by saying this to him. You are protecting his feelings, and your job, as well as his, is to do the very best you can to protect each other's feelings.

Mr. NewMan is better at everything than Mr. Ex, even if Mr. Ex was a rocket scientist who invented nanobot technology that saved millions of lives. If your ex happens to be famous and has accomplished a lot and Mr. NewMan knows this, you can make Mr. NewMan feel secure by telling him one of the things Mr. Ex wasn't good at and didn't accomplish was getting you and making you happy—like Mr. NewMan is doing.

If Mr. NewMan is also divorced, he's going to be more cautious this time around because he 'failed' once and doesn't want to again. We men HATE to fail. Of course, there is no such thing as failure until you quit trying to accomplish something you still want to accomplish. But he feels like he failed.

What if you're divorced and have kids? A friend of mine, Lisa, is two-years-divorced and has a six-year-old daughter. She told me that a lot of men will tune out and turn off the moment they hear she has a child. My advice was simple. Don't date this freakin' moron-face.

I told her to 007 him to see if he even likes kids and is comfortable having an instant family if things move forward. He'll lie to get into your pants, but the good thing is, you haven't let him into your pants yet, so you are seeing the real him and how he really feels about your daughter.

I also suggested that pictures around the house should be of her and her child; not her, her child and Mr. Ex. Any pictures like that should be in the child's room. If this guy has a problem with that and feels threatened by that—ex him.

Also, my personal feeling is a woman shouldn't introduce a man she's dating to her child until she is pretty damn sure this is a man she wants. This is not because of him; it's because of the child. This is not my area of expertise, but I imagine that most children would be confused if they met Mr. Now who becomes Mr. Then and suddenly, there is a new Mr. Now. Why not wait until Mr. Now has become Mr. Wow and you want to become Mrs. Wow.

No woman needs a man. Most want a man (or partner). Don't look at your first (or second, third, fifth) marriage as failure. Look at it (or them) as learning experiences. As Mary Pickford (actress, trailblazer and one of the founders of United Artist) said, *"If you have made mistakes… there is always another chance for you… you may have a fresh start any moment you choose, for this thing we call 'Failure' is not the falling down, but the staying down."* Or, to put it in simple man grunt, *"You're never down until you're out."*

POINT VALUE: Plus ten if you make him feel safe. Minus ten if he thinks Mr. Ex is still in your heart.

FOR THE SIX MEN READING THIS BOOK: If she's friends with an ex—don't alienate him. He could be a wealth of information. If you meet a woman who has kids, don't expect her to put your feelings above her children ever, and certainly not at the start of the relationship. As time goes by, things will balance out, but I suspect and hope the kids always come first. If you're the kind of guy that isn't into a woman who has kids, let her know this at the get-go, so she can look for another man who is. If you don't, you're a real motherfucker in every bad sense of the word.

203

Tall Tales

Enjoy His Stories and He Will Enjoy Being
Around You

"The enthusiasm of a woman's love is even beyond the biographer's."

— Jane Austen

ALTHOUGH men would prefer to just grunt and beat our chests; these days, that doesn't work like it did in Cave Town. So, we've substituted that with telling our 'war' stories. Whether it's about the big deal he just made at work, or past victories during glory days of playing ball, or, "Look, honey, I put together the new barbecue! All by myself... what, these pieces still sitting on the ground? They must be extras." Make him feel good about himself.

This is one of those times men LOVE to talk and go into details. Why? Ego. Oh, and there's another reason. Ego. And one more. Ego. All three "egos" add up to wanting to feel good about himself, wanting to impress you so he feels good about himself, and mostly, wanting to be loved.

While he's talking, if you so desire, drift into Peanuts Land. Hear, "wa, wa, wa, wa, wa" while you're thinking of something else. Nod. Smile. Say, 'Wow!' Or 'Really!' Or 'That's amazing!'

Some men fear that they are going to run out of "war stories" and in doing so, lose the interest of their Fair Maiden.

It's not a bad idea to, every now and then, say to him, "Honey, can you tell me about the time you scored the winning touchdown again?"

Or, "Honey, can you tell me about the time you saved that woman's life when she almost died from that paper cut?"

Then act like you're interested. Better yet, find a way to be interested in his stories. Even if the only reason you are interested is that you know how happy it makes him to tell these stories.

POINT VALUE: Plus eight if you enjoy his endless stories! Minus nine if he sees you constantly rolling your eyes.

FOR THE SIX MEN READING THIS BOOK: After she has heard the story of you scoring the winning touchdown for the millionth time, don't expect her to get all impressed over it again. Also, do NOT be a dickhead. Telling stories of your victories is fine. Telling stories about your victories with other women is not.

Albert Einstein Failed Math

Sure He's an Idiot. But He's Your Idiot

"Love is the triumph of imagination over intelligence."
– H.L. Mencken
(One of America's most renowned reporters, critics, and political commentators)

IS it that big of a deal if, for a few hours, the capital of California is Los Angeles? Does it matter that much if he thinks you're going to visit the Leaning Tower of Pizza?

Don't make him look bad in front of his friends, his family, your friends, business associates, dog, fish, hermit crab, waiter, whomever else is around. It makes him feel less of a man, and no man wants to be with a woman who does this to him. I'm not saying to agree with him when you know he's wrong. I'm not saying if there is a friendly debate going on and you disagree with him you shouldn't. If your man can't handle that, find a better man. I'm saying so what if he doesn't know the little fork is for salad and not the soup? He'll eventually figure it out.

If you want to correct him, pull him aside or wait to say something when the two of you are alone.

"Honey, I think Tony Blair was the Prime Minister of England, not Tony the Tiger."

He'll appreciate that you knew he was wrong, yet didn't say anything in front of everyone.

When it comes to your man driving I suggest using Google Maps. (Little known fact that during his voyage across the sea to India, Columbus wouldn't listen to his wife, who suggested that he pull over and ask for directions.)

Say, "I'm your wingman."

He'll not only understand that because it's Movie Speak, but he'll also be happy that you understand him and movie speak!

Remember that fragile ego of his. He thinks he knows everything, he knows that he doesn't, but he hates it if anyone else finds out. You're a team. No need to air your laundry in public.

POINT VALUE: Plus nine if you let things slide until later. Minus ten if you feel the need to constantly correct him in front of other people.

FOR THE SIX MEN READING THIS BOOK: You're an idiot. Have you listened to some of the lame ass, dumb ass, completely, absolutely wrong stupid crap that comes out of your mouth? You don't know it all. Not even close. Stop acting like you do, because if you admit you don't, you'll actually learn something. Triple/Double, Dude, triple/double. The smartest people in the world know what they don't know. Be one of those smartest people. Oh, and on one of those many car rides, when you finally get home after being lost because you wouldn't listen to her, apologize for getting mad when she told you to turn left.

Tammy Wynette, Your Man

> "Stand by Your Man." By Doing So, You Will Capture His Mind, Body, Heart and Soul

> *"The big difference between people is not rich or poor or good or evil... The biggest difference is between those who've had pleasure in love and those who haven't."*
> – From "Sweet Bird of Youth."
> Play by Tennessee Williams
> (One of America's greatest playwrights).
> Screenplay by Richard Brooks
> (One of America's greatest filmmakers).
> Spoken by Paul Newman
> (One of America's greatest human beings)

IF the man you want is a 'career man', understand what his career means to him. Understand his career is extremely important to him. Understand it goes to the very core of who he is—it defines him.

Don't expect him to put you above it right away. Chances are he's been working at it longer than he's known you. Even after a while, it might seem he cares more about his career than you. In no way does that mean he isn't madly in love with you and wouldn't be lost without you. (Very few men have soared the heights of career ecstasy without a woman at their side who, in all probability, is in front of him clearing the path to lead the way) It means that *men have an instinctual need to be the provider*.

It's a habit. Goes all the way back to the time when we first existed. But again, the good news is, this is yet another of *his habits you can use to your advantage*.

Which brings me to another point: I do not believe if a man has a limited amount of time to see you, it means he doesn't want you, care about you, or love you. It's not that black and white. It could mean that he's very busy building and/or maintaining his career. When he gives himself a break, if he wants that break to be with you, you must be very important to him. If he's taking breaks and is consistently not spending that time with you—then, it's time for you to put on the breaks, break-free and look for a new man to break-in. I mean get. Hmmm… kinda the same thing, don't you think?

A woman who understands late hours, changing date night, doing work at home, dealing with emergencies when the two of you were supposed to be together, deadlines, drive, ambition, the need to succeed, the need to be focused—is a true TeamMATE. He sees in you a partner that can help him achieve his career goals and his life goals.

If your guy is career driven, you will lose major points if you do not understand this about him. But why wouldn't you understand this about him? You had to know how driven he was before you decided you wanted to get him. Why fight one of the forces that you were attracted to in the first place?

My friend Nadal is a very driven guy. He worked very hard to get where he's at and he's still not where he wants to be. Within three seconds, you can see this about him. He dated a woman named Flip-Flop. Flip-Flop and he had a great thing going. She was totally there for him when, many times, he needed to be at work and was not with her. She totally understood his desire and passion for his career. She would say how much she loved that about him. They got married and all was right with the world!

But then something changed a year or so into the marriage. Flip-Flop no longer liked that Nadal was so passionate and focused on his career. She wanted him around more often. She wanted more of his time. Yet, she went into the relationship knowing what Nadal was like, and that was part of the reason she loved him. Needless to say, Flip-Flop went from being a teamMATE Nadal wanted to play with to a teammate he couldn't wait to trade. Know the man you're with. If he is career driven, chances are he always will be. If it's something you love about him but you can't deal with in the long run, then it's best for you to move on. You don't want to waste your time. If it bothers you to build your life with a man who wants to build his career and at times, puts it above all else, including you, you'll be miserable. Open a new door.

If, however, he is a career-driven kind of guy and you understand that about him, stand by your man. If he's a good man, and why would you want to be with anything less, he will most certainly stand by you—at the altar... and for a lifetime.

POINT VALUE: + *off the charts* for a woman who understands her man and is fine with being there for him.

FOR THE SIX MEN READING THIS BOOK:

1. Many women are incredibly passionate about their careers. If those women didn't exist, the world would be a much, MUCH emptier place. Those women would like a man to stand by them. If she's career driven and you can't deal with that, don't waste her time. Move on. Otherwise, stand by your woman.

2. If you're career driven, and she's fine with that, don't forget how driven she is to help you attain your goals. Plan a date night once in a while. When you have free time, spend it with her and show her how much you love her. She understands you and is on her side. You need to understand her and be on her side. Reassure her how important she is to you. Let her know that, without her, none of what you've accomplished matters. She's your team MATE. You're MVP. You know how important an MVP is to a team. Show her that.

Remember, the greatest thing in life is to find something you love to do—and someone you love to share it with.

You don't want to live half a life, do you?

Stress Test

Don't Add Stress to His Life

(Question) *"What kind of woman do you want to marry?"*
(Answer) *"One who doesn't annoy me."*
— Joe DeMarco
(The great, late VP of Fox Searchlight.
Built the studio into one of the greatest
independent studios of all time.)

MANY men feel like Atlas with the world on their shoulders (not realizing it is really women who are Atlas). Unless you're with a guy who loves drama, and why would you want to be, the last thing any man wants or needs is to be stressed out when it comes to being in a relationship. I'm sure you feel the same way. Life is stressful enough. Most men put a lot of pressure on themselves, which causes stress. His relationship with you should relieve stress—not cause it.

Look at a relationship like catching the perfect wave. When you see one you want, you're excited beyond. When you first catch it, you're a kid in a candy store. As you ride it, you still have passion doing so. You know at times it's going to be smooth and perfect. You know there will be moments when it will be choppy and difficult. But you're willing to do the work, to stay on this wave because you know when you come out of that choppy time, you're back in heaven. You know that you have to work it to make it work, but it's well worth because most of the time it's stress-free and happy—you don't want that wave to ever end. You wish you could ride it your entire life.

Be that wave.

Watch his patterns so you know when he's stressed out, then you can help him relieve it. He not only wants this from you, *he expects it from you*. It's *INSTINCTUAL*.

Remember, it was a woman from the start that relieved his stress long ago. Every time he was hungry, he got that great womb service. Even after he was evicted, there's a good chance it was still a woman who fed him when he was hungry and held him when he was scared.

If you can relieve his stress, you become a woman who, whenever he thinks of you, thinks of how wonderful you make him feel—even when he's not feeling so wonderful.

He thinks of you as his MVP.

Guys know that MVP's are very, *VERY* hard to come by. That's because they raise the bar, so those around them raise their game. When a man finds an MVP—*he's going to do all he can to make sure she stays on his team.*

SUBCONSCIOUS POINT VALUE: Again, *plus off the chart* if you don't add stress to his life. Plus beyond off the charts if you help relieve his stress. Minus off the chart if you make is life more stressful

FOR THE SIX MEN READING THIS BOOK: You don't have to hide your emotions all the time. Let her know when you're stressed out. Talk with her before that steam boils over. She's your MVP. Who better to help you get through it?

What All Men Are Ultimately Looking For

A Man Wants a Woman Who Can Bring Out the
Best in Him So He Can Be a Better Man

"You make me want to be a better man."
– Jack Nicholson
(In "As Good As It Gets."
Written by Mark Andrus and James L. Brooks)

IN a script I wrote, called "For God and Country", I described the lead female character this way: "She's the kind of woman you can spend all night making love to, all day hanging out with and a lifetime knowing she's got your back."

I actually got calls from a lot of fellow grunters who read that script saying they love the description. At the time I wrote it, I thought it was pretty basic. What I forgot is that it IS basic and it IS what all men want.

A man doesn't want to be changed. He wants to be accepted for who he is… with all his many flaws he knows he has better than anyone else. He wants you to understand him, even when he doesn't understand himself. He wants you to forgive him for the dumb mistakes he's going to make. He wants you to see in him things he won't reveal to others… even sometimes to you. He wants you to bring out in him those things he knows are there but haven't fully bloomed.

In a movie called "In Good Company", written and directed by Paul Weitz, Topher Grace asks Dennis Quaid, "What does it take to make a marriage work?"

His answer: "First, you have to find the right person to be in the foxhole with."

This answer goes for both men and women.

When you find Mr. Right, he's thinking whether you're the woman he wants to be in the foxhole with. Both consciously and subconsciously. (Of course, you should also ask yourself if he's the man you want in your foxhole. Uh, that didn't come out right. Wait! Maybe it did!)

A man wants a woman who makes his world less complicated and makes his life easier and more rewarding. He wants a woman to make him feel like he's in heaven, even at times when it seems like he's in hell.

Remember, "The closest a man will ever get to Heaven on Earth... is by being with a woman."

You and you alone hold the key to that elusive gate. Open it for him by understanding how to operate him, how to use his instincts and habits to both his advantage and yours... and he will want to walk arm-in-arm with you through those gates—and beyond.

POINT VALUE: There is no number high enough to explain how valuable any woman like this is to a man, lucky enough to have her want him.

TO YOU SIX MEN READING THIS BOOK: I know
exactly what you're thinking; 'Amen, brother.' Amen indeed.

Q-Tips

"It is not enough that we do our best; sometimes we have to do what's required."
– Sir Winston Churchill
(One of Britain's Greatest Prime Ministers)

THESE are quick tips that will get you more points in the 'PRO' column of that yellow legal pad, because every advantage you can gain, even little ones, are huge.

1   Most men want to be the most important person in your world, but he doesn't want to be your entire world. He'll start to feel like he can't breathe. He'll start to feel guilty about doing things without you and start to resent you. (Remember, men love their space.) Have a life outside of your man. Have interests and things you like to do on your own or with your friends. Not only does this help your relationship, but it also helps you. Because then he's not the only thing that shapes and defines who you are.

2   When buying your man a gift, buy him something that shows him you actually know who he is and what he likes. Sounds simple? Apparently not. I can't begin to tell you how many gifts I have received from women I have dated, and I wonder, "Why did she think I'd like this?" I do remember the few times I got great gifts. I'm not talking about expensive gifts, many of the expensive ones sucked too. I'm talking about buying him something that shows him you took the time to really see who he is. Like if he has a Bugs Bunny cell, mug and t-shirt (like me); he might appreciate a Bugs Bunny bathrobe instead of a Beauty and the Beast soap dish.

3   Speaking of great gifts, buy your man a grill. Yes, we love it when you cook for us, but barbecuing is an activity we enjoy. There's something about it that makes us want to cook. Unlike an oven, we throw the meat on the grill. GRUNT! We see the flames. GRUNT! We see danger! GRUNT! GRUNT! We watch it cook. GRUNT! GRUNT! GRUNT!!! So, a great gift for you to give you—I mean him—is a grill. It's the gift that keeps on giving. He'll enjoy using it and you'll enjoy letting him use it. Triple/Double.

4   We don't consider a day of shopping to be fun, fun, fun!

5   We hate coasters.

6   We don't understand throw pillows.

7   We hate doilies.

8   This is an oldie, but a goodie. From a very early age, we boys are taught to put the seat up when we have to pee. So, it became a habit. But not one man I asked, not a one, said he was taught to put it back down. So, leaving it up became part of the 'putting it up' habit. I'm just as guilty as most guys and I grew up with four women and one bathroom. (Often, I'd hear my name being yelled when one of my sisters went to sit down and ended up splashing down.) If someone with my background still makes this mistake too often, why complain about something you know isn't going to change? It's a force of nature—like the way you feel about shoes.

9   If your man has a dog, love his dog! The same goes for his parrot, turtle, hermit crab, pot-belly pig, or cat, 'cause if he owns it, he loves it and so should you. If he owns a snake, you can love it from a distance. If he owns a cat it doesn't mean he's gay, but he could be an evil villain.

10 There is something really sexy about a woman wearing a hat every now and then. A baseball cap, or a do-rag, pirate style. I don't know why. Maybe it's because we think you will get a little rougher and tumble when sex is involved. You know, the way we did in Cave Town. Or, maybe the hat thing is just me. I do like that Santa hat after all.

11 Speaking of 'rough and tumble', we enjoy it if, from time-to-time, when you're "one of the guys" and are not afraid to get "down and dirty" with us. Play in the rain and mud.

Get a little greasy with us under that car. Hit the gym together. Shoot some hoops. Play some tennis. Sometimes, it's sexy to get sweaty. (There is one downside to this, however. If you live together, and maybe even if you don't, when all is said and done—yep, you got it. He's going to toss those muddy, greasy, sweaty things in a pile on your floor.)

12 Don't expect him to pay the tab. *Appreciate* it when he does. Call me old-fashioned, but as I said before, I believe the man is the one who should pay. (In Europe I've actually had women get pissed at me for wanting to pay. As much as American women claim to want equal rights, doesn't seem to be the case at all in when it comes to buying the drinks or the meal, because never once in America has that happened to me or any guy I know). However, I can't begin to tell you how much a turn-off it is when I take a woman out and she doesn't thank me. She loses major points. Also, every once in a while, offer to pay. It doesn't have to be fancy; it can be a couple of burgers. Or offer to go Dutch. (Are Dutch men that cheap?) It shows you're a team player. Even if he won't let you pay or go Dutch, he will appreciate that you offered. If he does pay, send him a text or email thanking him. You'll score points.

13 Like I said earlier, around 40% of the women in The United States y make more money than their husbands (And that's earning 70+ cents to a man's dollar). If you make more money than your man, you have to make him feel like a man. Why? Goes back to Cave Town. Remember, men instinctively are the providers, women are the nurturers. Let him know there are things he does for you that no amount of money can buy. I have dated women who make more money than me or came from a lot more money than me and it didn't really matter to me. There was one relationship in particular I was really into. I felt we could go all the way. She made a lot more money than I did and came from money as well. As our relationship moved forward, she started to make me feel uncomfortable. Little things about money would come up from her. Trips she wanted to take but was unwilling to

219

go Dutch if it was too expensive for me to pay for the both of us. I didn't like feeling "unmanly" so I moved on. Most men, unless they are a hustler, will do the same. If you really like the guy and want to make it work, let him feel that, although he doesn't bring as much bread to the table as you do, he still brings a lot to the table.

14 Hair flipping, back arching, and pouting your lips (as long as it's not about pouting) are damn sexy! Those images can burn in our minds and get to our hearts.

15 Many men don't like making the bed. In our minds, it's going to get messy like 16 hours later, so why bother?

***

That being said, when I dated Roz, she went to work before me. She asked me to make the bed, several times. I gave her the above excuse. She didn't ask anymore. Then I thought to myself, *Self, am I that big of an asshole that I can't take one and a half minutes to do something she'd like?* I made the bed. I can't begin to tell you how happy that made her. I scored major points. Not because I made the bed, but because I did something that meant something to her. I put her feelings above my selfishness. This last paragraph was for the six men reading this book.

16 We know the elastic on that pair of underwear is shot, those socks have worn thin, and that shirt is near death. We just don't want to get rid of them. Why? "Cause retro's in!" Okay, it has nothing to do with retro. We keep them because we really don't care about fashion. (According to my sisters, and pretty much any woman I ever dated, left to my own accord, I am a fashion disaster.) When we dress nicer it's because we get a positive reaction from women. (Yet another example of how men do everything to get a woman and why you have so much power to get what you want from a man.) Otherwise, we'd be more than happy to wear styles that haven't been in for 300 years and white in fall. As long as what we are wearing is comfortable—and easily reached in that pile

220

near the bed, we're happy. Unlike you and your shoes, we prefer comfort over style and these old 'rags' are so darn comfortable. If you need to say something to us about our worn-out clothes, just say, "I love that little quirk about men, it's what makes you men." Your man will be thrilled that you understand him. Then, if you want, buy him new stuff. He's still not going to throw out the old stuff, but he will eventually get to the new stuff and forget about the old stuff.

17 Talk the walk. What I mean by this is, too often the lack of communication ends a relationship. Speak up. (Make sure it's at a time when you have his full attention). Don't let it fester. Be open and honest with him *and yourself.* That way you have a much better chance of walking the talk down the aisle and down the road of life together.

18 Studies show that married men live longer and are healthier than single men. Now, I'm not suggesting that you should tell your man this as a way to get him to marry you. I am certainly not saying that scaring him into marriage is the way to go. But, so what if you happen to place magazines with these facts some place, he might read them. Like, ya' know, the bathroom. Okay, I'm just having fun with this one. You really don't want to scare anyone into marrying you. Not a way to build a solid foundation for a lasting relationship. That being said, married men do live longer and healthier lives. (As far as you six men reading this book goes, did you know that studies show that married men live longer and healthier lives?)

Part V
Final Thoughts

If I Only Knew Then What I Know Now

"Advantage is something you seek for pleasure, or even for profit, like a gold rush or invading a country; but experience is what really happens to you in the long run; the truth that finally overtakes you."

–Katherine Anne Porter
(Pulitzer Prize winning writer)

"A discovery is said to be an accident meeting a prepared mind."

– Albert von Szent-Gyorgyi
(Hungarian born scientist)

'Love is everything it's cracked up to be… It really is worth fighting for, being brave for, risking everything for."

– Erica Jong

Or as the singer Jimmy Buffett said:

"Some people claim that there's a woman to blame, but I know it's my own damn fault."

ONE of the catalysts that got me to write this book was this one particular woman I dated a long time ago. I'm not really sure I knew that until just now. I, like you, have discovered things during this journey. I, like you, have become even more aware of what I already knew, and have learned things I didn't know.

This particular woman came very close to getting me. I was young, dumb and full of…stupidity. I was the one who screwed it up. I truly believe, from the bottom of my heart, if she had the information in this book, we would have gotten married.

Please understand I am not blaming her for our demise. I don't blame others for my mistakes. I blame myself. I HATE when people don't take responsibility. It's a pet peeve of mine. As Oprah Winfrey (survivor, talk show host, actress, philanthropist, Self-made billionaire and champion of equal rights), said, *"I don't think of myself as a poor, deprived ghetto girl who made good. I think of myself as somebody who, from an early age, knew I was responsible for myself, and I had to make good."* Being responsible for one's self also means you take the blame when you do wrong, and more than likely those who helped you do right. (If only America's 45th president understood this, the world would be a better and safer place. Perhaps we will get lucky and America's 46th president will feel this way. Perhaps she will even be the one who said this quote. Hey, one can dream!)

So why do I say I blew it and then say if she had read this book, we would be married? Because then she would have had a guide and the tools that showed her how to think like a man and operate one; me. She would have had instructions that would have enlightened me as to what I had with her and what I didn't want to lose. Her. She would have had a book to toss at my head when I was being stupid and get me to be one of the six men reading this book to help me remember all she does for me, and remind me how hard it would be to go back out there and good luck finding another woman, who does all the things she does, who I have this kind of chemistry with.

Thus, another reason I realize that I wrote this book. I don't want two people who have something incredibly special with someone amazingly special to blow it. Like I did.

For you six men reading this, when you find 'The One', don't let fear dictate your moves. Take the chance—give it your all. Don't be a toad. Make her feel like the princess she is. Show her she is the most important person in your life because you are the most important person in hers. Be there for her because she will be there for you. Trust her with your heart, because she has given you hers.

Take the chance. Dive into the deep end of the pool.

If you don't, you'll realize what you lost. Then you'll run back and dive in heart full—only to crash head first. Because by then... the pool will be empty.

Final Thoughts

"One of the things about equality is not just that you be treated equally to a man, but that you treat yourself equally to the way you treat a man."

– Marlo Thomas
(Actor, advocate, 'That Girl')

THANK YOU for spending this time with me. I hope you are happy that you read this book and that you enjoyed the journey. You have learned the truth about men, and how to think like a man. In doing so, you have the information you need to understand what makes up a man. Now that you know how he thinks, what he thinks and why he thinks the way he does—you are empowered to operate him, get him, and successfully make him yours.

Please put what you have learned or relearned to practical use. So many people learn something and then never use that knowledge. Knowledge = power, but only if put to use. If not used, it's just wasted knowledge. In this case, it's also wasting the natural gifts Mother Nature empowered you with.

I hope you have learned never to forget or diminish the power you hold in your heart. The power you have to get a man. The power you have over men. The power you have to make your life what you want it to be.

When it comes to that man you want, I hope you know your own self-worth and choose a man who deserves you. As Janis Joplin said, "Don't compromise yourself. You are all you've got."

I hope you find true, lasting love. For with it, comes pure happiness, which is better than all the Prada bags, Gucci shoes, diamond bracelets, corporate takeovers, Academy

Awards, business lunches, hip party invites, and summer houses one can own.

To be able to share love is to be able to have a lifetime of shared moments. If you sat down to think about all the moments you've had in your life, you could probably do it in 24 hours. That's a <u>lifetime</u> of moments remembered in 24 hours. That's why when those moments are shared with that one person who means more to you than anyone else, you have a wealth that can never, ever be taken away or equaled. You have a history you can live in the present... and beyond.

Above all, remember, any man who has a special woman in his life is blessed. For you are what all MANkind seeks.

You are the Holy Grail.

Acknowledgments

Gambaru: *"Never, ever, ever give up. Especially when you have no chance of winning"*
— Japanese saying

MY gratitude is unbound for all the women I've ever encountered as friends or lovers, and in doing so, gave me the reason to write this book.

There are people that, over my life, affected me in a positive way that changed my life. Sometimes it was something they said. Other times something they did. Sometimes in small ways, that lead to huge changes. Other times more obvious. On my journey that is life, these people have helped shape who I am, thus making this book possible. I can in no way name them all, and I apologize to those I have left out. Here are but a few people I'd like to single out:

Tom Arnold, Kevin Bacon, Billy Barshop, Kylie Bax, Evan Berk, Corbin Bernsen, Maurice Benard, Gerrie Biegner, Malcolm Bird, Marlon Brando, Nikki Carvey, John Scott Cook, Cami Curtis, George Clooney, Dan Cortese, Dabney Coleman, Loretta Colla, Cindy Crawford, Leslie Danon, Lauren Shuler Donner, Hilary Duff, Margaret Easley, Erik Estrada, Jeff Garlin, Eric Gold, Patrick Hughes, Lindsay Varner-Kirkman, Mila Kunis, Wendy L'Belle, Heidi Van Lier, Steve Lordson, Peter Lovello, Julia Luppino, Stephen Lynch, Annette Marquez, Margaret Kathryn Molloy, Julie Moran, Rob Moran, Julia Myrick, Kris Nicolau, Mark O'Mera, Lolia Peralta, Kelly Preston, Kirk Stambler, Payne Stewart, Victoria Tennant, Gene Wilder, and Robin Williams.

"Excuse me! Did you say you wanted to thank 'A few people?' This is not a few people!" I know, I know. But this is my first published book and well... Catherine, Monica, Debbie,

229

Diane, Emily, Hannah, Holly, Jessica, Jillian, Joan, Joanne, Karen, Kim, Dawn, Lydia, Randi, Maria, Michele, RoseMarie, Shannon, Shari, Sherry, Shevonne, Stacey, Susan, and Trinee Lucky Nickel, Seltzer, Beethoven, Sundance, Bowie

Lucky Nickel, Seltzer, Beethoven, Sundance, Bowie

Me. Fishy, Smoosh, Maggie, Monster, Clamenza, and El Gato.

"Excuse me. Did you just thank your pets?" Yes, yes, I did. We can learn a lot from our pets and the "animal" kingdom. Many times, they are more human than we are.

Grandma Elsie, Grandpa Mac, Grandma Silvia, Grandpa Chappie, Aunt Beverly, Uncle Avie, Aunt Janet, Uncle Phil, Aunt Francie, Uncle Stevie and Aunt Thelma. Cousins Candy, Laura. Richard, Sara, Stephen, and Susan. Inés Dominguez Barrena, Jon Cohen, Daniel Garridodepedro, Lorraine Lages, Dan Schloss, Didi Garcia-Serrano, Mireia "Sunday" Garcia-Serrano, Alan "Doc" Spiegel, Lili Spiegel, Anne Spiegel, Dr. Tesler, Nancy Tesler, Leo Bookman, Raymond DeMarco, Cherie DeMarco, Julian DeMarco, Edurne Dominguez, Charlie Durden, Jose Luis "The Great Caruto" Fernandez, Bobby Jurkoskis, Peter Sanchez,

I'd like to totally thank; Stan Lee, Dave Chapelle, Julie Adams, Dave Alpert, Ivie Anderson, Rebecca "The Beckster" Bennett, Emil Buyse, Evan Chandler, Lisa Carfano, William "Rock" Dozier, Cary Elwes, Andrew Erin, Meg Fein, Brad Fuller, Frank Fraboni, Jessica Green, Rich Green, Kevin Hassarud, Steven Hentges, Alfonso "Fonzi" Antolín Hernández, Karen Hollander, Greg Judge, Nick Kallsen, Richard Kilstock, Jon Kobrin,, Alyssa Manner Kogon, Joe Kraemer, Marco Lagana, Charlie Barrington Lewis, Richard Lewis, Sir George Lucas, Philip Luppino, John Mass, Dan Mirvish, Andy Miller, John Moffit, Dan Myrick, Richie Pola, Aaron Priest, Greg Prusak, Nick Reed, Roger Rees, Mitzi Shore, Steve Simeone, David Spiegelman, Margaux St. Ledger, Susie Watson Taylor, Adam Toft, John Travolta, Duncan Trussell, Plato Wang, Coach Williams, Brian Woods, Stephen Zakman, and Dani Zoldan.

"Excuse me. You're the one who said, 'Land the plane.' Does this look like landing the plane to you?" Okay, you make a good point. I'm not exactly landing the plane here. "Hey, Mr. Ungettable, have you thought about writing a book just thanking people? 'Cause this is what this is turning into!" Fear not, we at the final stretch. I'd like to especially thank: Michael Blaha, Ellen Chopay, Joe DeMarco, Meredith Karasch, Daniella Rich-Kilstock, Joey Lee Kirkman, Nevra, Fay Masterson, Donna Moffit, Adam Novak, Maryann Roberts, Daron Rosenberg, Gary Spiegel, Ken Tesler, and Richard X.

My sisters Karen, Nancy, and Pam. My mother, Barbara. My father, Robert.

My first-grade teacher, Mrs. Green, who didn't give me minus points for my bad spelling, because, as she said to my mother, "He's very creative, and I'm worried if I penalize him for his spelling, he won't want to write." She was my angel on Earth, one of many.

A very special thanks and shout out to Melissa Morris, my publicist. Without her passion and belief in me, this book would have never been published. In fact, she is the one who got it to publishers and generated interest.

I want to thank the good people at Austin Macauley Publishers for having the foresight and courage to publish this book. I also want to thank Patrick Silverthorn for the Cover Design/Art and Tony Chargin for the doodle drawings.

I want to thank the many, MANY people who told me "no," "impossible," "you'll never amount to anything" and things like that. You fueled me and ignited the fire within me.

I'd also like to thank you and every woman who, in spite of everything, still believes in romance and still believes they will find happily ever after... For love is the magical whisper that makes life worth living. Last, but certainly in no way least, I want to thank Elisabeth. She opened a world, both inside of me and out, that empowered me to overcome some fears, open my heart and take risks I never thought I was capable of taking. Because of her love, friendship, and great intelligence I am forever a changed and better man.

Gambaru!!!

Author's Postscript

"There came a time when the risk to remain tight in the bud was more painful than the risk it took to blossom."
— Anaïs Nin

I once wrote a screenplay in a week and sold it to Warner Brothers three days later. I'm not telling you this to brag. I'm letting you know this, because some stories can flow while others swim upstream; neither of which makes the story any better or worse. Each story has its own path, and the person writing that story MUST let the story dictate how it flows, not try to force the direction of the flow. Otherwise the work is not fully honest and therefore not worth being seen, heard or read. This book took me a very long time to write. Fifteen years or so. I'd write, put it down for a while to incubate, go back to it and write some more. I even put it down for a several years because something wasn't working for me in the book; I wasn't sure what it was, and I wanted to make sure I got this book right. I finally realized what wasn't working, fixed it, and am very proud to have this book being published. It also took a long time because I had my 'day job' as a screenwriter and director, family matters to deal with, personal responsibilities that came my way, etc. etc. Or as John Lennon said, "Life is what happens while you're planning other things." Another reason it took a while is, as you know, I'm Dyslexic. So, my spelling and grammar are atrocious beyond! It took ten thousand people to go through my manuscript to catch all my mistakes; and they didn't catch several (My publicist Melissa Morris caught one prior to publishing). I've decided to keep some—wouldn't feel right if I wrote something completely mistake free. Okay, okay, it wasn't ten thousand people. But it was a small and dedicated army who cursed me out as they fixed my mistakes but thanked me after having read the book.

Once Austin Macauley became my publisher, there were some edits, and of course more spelling and grammar mistakes fixed. During this time, I made a few revisions to this book prior to publication. Mostly tweaks and some minor updates. (My publisher and publicist will be thrilled I'm done, because I tend to tweak a lot even when they send back just spell/grammar corrections. Whether you're a writer, director, painter, sculpture, poet, builder, etc. no one ever finishes their work. They are pulled from it. Fighting tooth and nail all the way)

I gave copies of my manuscript to around 200 women and about a dozen men. What you are reading is about 97% of what they read.

So, even if I sell only one copy, and it helps the woman who bought it land a man I will be beyond happy I spent the time and energy to write Think Like a Man – The Only Guide You'll Ever Need. After all, like I've said in this book, a pebble in the ocean can create a tidal wave of change. And with all that has happened due to #Metoo, #Timesup and a strong contingency of women now in government positions and gaining more power in companies and at home—I'm very excited to see this tidal wave engulf us, because I fully believe it will last, it will get stronger, and it will be great for the world we live in.

Thank you.

jD Shapiro

Chivalry for the Six Men
Reading This Book

King Arthur looks at the one empty seat at the Not So Round Table: "Where is Chivalry?" Suddenly, a guard BURSTS into the room: "My King. Chivalry is dead." CUT TO various scenes of men suddenly being unchivalrous: 1) A man pulls a chair AWAY from the woman about to sit in it. She falls to the ground. 2) A man pulls the coat off the puddle he just put it over. A woman steps into the puddle and sinks to her neck. 3) A woman walks into her house carrying four heavy bags of groceries, her twins, both car seats and a kitchen sink. A man sits on the couch, feet up, watching a soccer match. MAN: "Hey, can you get me some chips, guac, and three beers already? I've been sitting here for hours waiting."
    – Scene from: *"King Arthur & His Knights of the Not So Round Table".*

WHAT'S old again is new again. Like men being confused during the first women's movement in the 1970s, they are back to being confused again about how to act. So, here are my personal rules of chivalry:

OPEN THE FREAKIN' DOOR: Building door, house door, office car door, etc. Sure, there might be some women who are offended by it because we men think they can't do it for themselves (for the record, I don't know any man who don't think a woman can open a door by herself. Yet, they want us to hold their purses…?) It's the polite and nice thing to do because there is still valor in life and should always be.

GIVE UP YOUR SEAT: This one might get you more pushback than holding open the door, but again, I think it's the right thing to do. She probably works harder than you, then heads home and works even harder, and she might have to wear those torture shoes, what do you call them? Oh, right, High heels. You try standing in them all day. Or for ten minutes. (Actually, I need to try that. I have no idea what it is like, but I can imagine it suckkkkkkks). Hey, this is one area men ARE smarter than women! We ain't wearing those.

HELP HER: onto the boat, out of the car, into the car, etc. etc. etc. Maybe she is stronger than you but again, why not give her a helping hand because The Universe knows your out-of-shape ass wants some help but is too afraid to ask 'cause it's not manly.

STAND WHEN SHE LEAVES: This is a tricky one 'cause most people are going to look at you like you're an idiot. But I think it's a nice thing to do because it's a sign of respect and women deserve our respect as much as the men and women who serve our military. They are our first line of defense against ourselves.

SEE HER TO HER DOOR AND MAKE SURE SHE GETS INSIDE: There are bad people out there. If you care, make sure she doesn't have to deal with any of them on the way home. Again, she might have a carry permit and be the greatest shooter in the world. But, two is better defense than one in most situations.

Those are the main things that, for me, are still important and nice to do. There are things I believe men should do including helping with heavy packages, but I can't go into the minor list. I have to stop writing now because I promised Melissa Morris, my publicist, that I would be done by midnight so we can get this to the publisher by their time today (They are in London, I am presently in NYC). I like to keep my promises. And if you know Melissa, you don't want to get on her bad side. So, I'll end by saying to the Six Men Reading This Book, your woman deserves a man who can be a gentleman and gallant.

NOTE: My using a scene from the FANTASTIC script, "King Arthur & His Knights of the Not So Round Table" is called a "Shameless plug." 'Tis because it is—I wrote that fantastic script, soon to be in a movie theater near you! Once I get the money to finance it, that is. Anyone interested? Not an expensive movie and will be lots of fun! (That is known as Filmmaking 101: Ask anyone and everyone for money for an indecent movie). FYI Warren Beatty got on his knees and begged the studio chief to let him make, *Bonnie & Clyde*.